THE TEACHING of JUDAICA in AMERICAN UNIVERSITIES

The Proceedings of a Colloquium

Publication of this volume was assisted by a grant from Philip H. Lown, benefactor of the Philip H. Lown Graduate Center for Contemporary Jewish Studies at Brandeis University.

THE TEACHING of JUDAICA in AMERICAN UNIVERSITIES

The Proceedings of a Colloquium

edited by

LEON A. JICK

ASSOCIATION FOR JEWISH STUDIES

KTAV PUBLISHING HOUSE, INC.

LIBRARY OF CONGRESS CATALOG CARD NUMBER: 72-135521
MANUFACTURED IN THE UNITED STATES OF AMERICA

TABLE OF CONTENTS

INTRODUCTION

LEON A. JICK
Brandeis University
Director of the Lown Graduate Center
and Dean of the College

1

IN the recent past the pursuit of Jewish studies was virtually unknown in secular American universities. Chairs at Harvard, Columbia, and Yale were occupied by distinguished Jewish scholars who pursued their studies and taught small bands of devoted students in virtual isolation from the broader currents of academic life. The Jewish "presence" on most college campuses was limited to student service organizations and an occasional lectureship, most often designed to provide apologetic information on the Jewish background of Christianity. Jewish learning was confined to the seminaries which devoted themselves almost exclusively to training congregational rabbis. Jewish culture—language, history, literature, philosophy, folklore, sociology—was treated as "extracurricular," apologetic, or parochial.

In the turbulent decade of the 1960's America passed from the era of the "return to religion" to the era of the "death of God" and the "secular city"; religious traditions, already de-mythologized, were de-theologized. At the same time a resurgence of ethnic consciousness (especially among Black Americans) and a growing quest for recognition of diverse cultural elements reinforced an already existent tendency for universities to broaden the scope of their offerings and to introduce heretofore neglected materials. Among the new arrivals on many campuses was the oldest of Western cultures, the Judaic.

The growth of Jewish studies in American universities in the past decade cannot be described as a "movement" since it was neither anticipated nor fostered. For a time it was hardly perceived. Finally, in the American Jewish Yearbook of 1966 a seminal article by Arnold Band[1] chronicled the growth of the field and reported on its state at that time. Since then, the development, further stimulated by student interest and pressure, has accelerated.

A number of organizations of Jewish scholars do exist, and scholars in the various areas of Jewish culture participate in the deliberations of their specific disciplines. However, there has not been a forum where all teachers of Judaica in universities could meet to discuss their work and the problems of their field. The need for such a forum has received increasing recognition in recent years, particularly in the articles of Allan Cutler.[2] Finally, with the assistance of a grant from Boston philanthropist and educational leader, Philip W. Lown, an advisory committee of academicians was convened to plan a colloquium dealing with the problems of the field and exploring future needs. Every effort was made to assure that the committee would be broadly representative of scholarly disciplines, ideological points of view, and geographical locations, and would, insofar as possible, reflect the diversity of the field. While the initiative was taken by the Lown Graduate Center for Contemporary Jewish Studies at Brandeis University, the Colloquium and subsequent developments are the product of this committee, its members and the colleagues who joined them.[3] A profound debt of gratitude is due to all of these devoted scholars and teachers as well as to Dr. Bernard Reisman, Associate Director of the Lown Graduate Center.

The Colloquium demonstrated the need for such meetings, to be open to all teachers and students in the field of Jewish studies. It provided an opportunity for an exchange of ideas and experiences as well as for personal and intellectual contact and interaction. The need for ongoing communication was deeply felt by all of the participants who decided to proceed with the establishment of the Association for Jewish Studies, thus providing a framework for continuous cooperation and for engaging the numerous problems which were raised.

This volume contains the substance of the major papers delivered at the first Colloquium, together with two articles of historical interest by Professors Samuel Sandmel and Harvie Branscomb, prepared at the request of Professor Jacob Neusner. It is hoped that the dissemination of these papers will not only provide useful information, but will stimulate interest in the field of Jewish studies and will strengthen the growing effort to enhance the quality and quantity of such studies in American universities.

NOTES

1. Arnold J. Band, "Jewish Studies in American Liberal Arts Colleges and Universities," *American Jewish Yearbook,* Vol. 67 (New York: 1966), pp. 3–30.
2. Allan Cutler, "An Agenda For American Jewish Scholarship," *The Jewish Spectator* (June 19, 1967), pp. 21–22.
3. ADVISORY COMMITTEE:

Arnold J. Band	Yochanan Muffs
Gerson Cohen	Jacob Neusner
Nahum Glatzer	Nahum Sarna
Irving Greenberg	Marshall Sklare
Baruch Levine	Isadore Twersky
	Leon A. Jick, *Chairman*

THE UNIVERSITY AND JEWISH STUDIES

Lou H. Silberman
Vanderbilt University
Hillel Professor of Jewish Literature
and Thought

THE place to begin our examination of the relationship between the university and Jewish studies may very well be *die alte Aula* of the University of Basel under the watchful gaze of the portraits of the five generations of Buxtorfs who served as professors of Hebrew in that notable academy. The reason for this choice is not difficult to determine. It was Johannes Pater, whose career provided the turning point in the study of Judaism by Christians, and Johannes Filius, of whom it was said, "non ovum ovo similius quam Buxtorf pater et filius," who brought the literature of the Jews, and not the Hebrew Bible alone, into the university. Although it was his interest in the Bible that was the source of the elder's concern, it was by no means its limit. Dogmatic disputes with Roman Catholics concerning the inerrancy of the Hebrew Bible and the *veritas, authentia, sinceritas et integritas codicum hebraicorum, hodiernorum* may have set these men off on their studies, but the results went far beyond the intention. When one reads through the list of their publications and the catalogue of the library they collected, of the Hebrew texts whose printing they sponsored, of the son's translation of *Moreh Nebukhim* and *Kuzari* into Latin, one realizes that their involvement in Jewish studies transcended the theological interests that originally motivated them. Zunz attributed to the father the beginnings of Hebrew bibliography. Johannes Senior corresponded with Jewish scholars all over the world and even wrung from the city council of Basel the right to have the Jew who served as corrector of his edition of the rabbinic Bible reside in his home. Indeed, his attendance at the circumcision of his house-scholar's son cost him one hundred gulden—the fine imposed upon him and upon his son-in-law for that dereliction. Incidentally, Braunschweig, the Jew, was fined four hundred gulden.

It was the interest of Buxtorf that, in Zunz's words, laid out the threefold direction of the cultivation of Jewish literature in the following century and a half: 1) grammatical, the study of Hebrew, Aramaic, and "rabbinic"; 2) antiquarian, concerned with the *realia* of Jewish life and the attempt to relate them to exegesis; 3) literary, occupied with authors and books. During those one hundred and fifty years, this

9

activity, although carried out by theologians for theological purposes was, again in Zunz's expression, "erstaunenswürdig." "The Talmud," he reported, "was not burnt but searched and studied." The younger Buxtorf was said to have read both the Palestinian and Babylonian Talmudim. Hebrew manuscripts were purchased for both private and public collections. Considerable parts of the Mishnah were translated into Latin— a task fulfilled by Wilhelm Surenhuys (1698), who added thereto the translation of Maimonides' and Bertinoro's commentaries—as were the philosophers noted above. The Englishmen, Edward Pococke and John Lightfoot—the one, Professor of Hebrew at Oxford, the other Master of St. Catherine's at Cambridge—continued the task of translation; the former with an edition of the Arabic text of six sections of Maimonides' Commentary on the Mishnah and a Latin translation; the latter with *Horae Hebriacae et Talmudicae*—talmudic parallels to the Gospels, I Corinthians, Acts, and some chapters of Romans.

Jewish theology was the center of interest of others including Voisin and Carpzov, while still others busied themselves with Kabbala, Jewish family and public law, history, geography, and antiquarian objects. Hackspan, who died in 1659, wrote concerning the widespread usefulness of rabbinic studies, while Otho produced a geographic dictionary of the teachers of the Mishnah. This development and interest began to turn bitter at the beginning of the eighteenth century with the appearance of the infamous *Entdecktes Judenthum* of Eisenmenger—the arsenal of anti-Semites of this day. Johann Christian Wolf's *Bibliotheca Hebraea,* published thereafter (1715-1733), listing all works printed in Hebrew and written by Jews (even those who had been baptized) may be said to sum up the efforts of the previous century, but it lacked any overview. It was, as Zunz wrote, the work of a statistician.

Although Jewish studies continued to occupy the interest of university scholars during a large part of the eighteenth century, they finally fell victim to the same spirit that shattered the remaining monuments of the Middle Ages. "Jewish studies," Zunz wrote, "bound up with theology, hate, and Latin, retreated into the background." In the end they, "belonging neither to classics nor orientalia, neither to philology nor political philosophy, all but vanished from the scene." Of the nineteenth century he wrote, "there is little useful to note." Political reaction in Germany included rejection of Jewish emancipation, so that "the culture of the noble patricians was as well marked by conscious ignorance of the Jews and their literature as by bigoted pietism." Even the Jews fell victim to this adverse judgment. Anxious to catch up with the world into which they had stumbled, they "sacrificed their religion to philosophy that had broken their chains and their literature to culture that had offered them aid." "If the Jews despised the basis of their historical existence and offered their tradition for sale for the sake of emancipation, it is not strange that Christian divines were ashamed of any connection with Jewish life and left its scholarship strictly alone." So Zunz.[1]

David Kaufmann of Budapest, writing in 1895—fifty years after Zunz —on "Die Vertretung der jüdischen Wissenschaft an den Universitäten,"[2] bemoaned the fact that, despite the efforts and productivity of Jewish scholarship in modern times, all carried on without "the favor of the mighty and the wealth of the state, the *universitas litterarum* offers no protection for its legitimate off-spring but only stifling and smothering shade." Because Jewish studies had not found or, rather, had not been granted a place in the university, the whole program of preliminary studies on which mastery of the field is built was not available. "Hier beginnt," he wrote sarcastically, "mit jedem Professor die Welt von Neuem"; but let it be remembered that the professors of whom he wrote were not Jews.

The body of his paper consisted of a close examination of the egregious errors of some contemporary non-Jewish scholars who were engaged in dealing with Jewish subject matter—in this case most particularly *genizah* materials. Its lengthy conclusion was an indignant attack upon the situation in which Jewish scholarship, although *universitätsfähig,* was still excluded from the academy. Given the state of Jewish learning among non-Jews, what would happen to Jewish literature, he asked, "wenn nicht zuffällig, ohne Verschulden der christlichen civilisation," Jews vanished from the world? "I know," he wrote, "that the name university originally was only applied to the national or student associations collectively . . . but the ideal to which we today apply the concept *universitas litterarum* reflects the claim that there is no question between heaven and earth concerning which at least one member of the body is not competent to speak. Yet only one literature and the history of one community, that which bore all the monotheistic religions in its womb, in whose soil is rooted the holiest concepts of mankind, from which spring the streams that even today turn the mills of all theological faculties, remains at the door, whilst the most recent, the youngest sprout of the natural sciences and humanities demands and receives permission to enter the palace of learning. The demand that Jewish theology [but he means far more] be incorporated as a faculty of the university is still—despite all that has been done—scoffed at as immature boyishness or romantic enthusiasm (unreife Knabenhaftigkeit, romantische Schwärmerei)."

Pressing his attack upon the pretensions of his contemporaries in the university Kaufmann wrote that, "all of his grammatical penetration and his historical training did not make it possible for Ewald to recognize a portion of the evening liturgy for the Feast of Tabernacles." Of Paul de Lagarde he commented, "[he] was about to discover the names of the Psalmists in the Psalms when—to his own amazement—the fullness of his linguistic preparation was disclosed when he tried to read a *piyyut*." In a biting sentence he noted, "Mommsen declared that prehistory is the only discipline in which one can dispense with knowledge of the alphabet. However," he continued, "among historical disciplines Jewish scholarship requires something more than the mere mastery of the Hebrew alphabet."

His goal was, however, not the exclusion but the inclusion of non-Jews into the fields of Jewish learning. ". . . Jewish scholarship is not an arcane discipline. The human mind has mastered more remote and abstruse subjects. But knowledge is born only out of love. Only to the farmer who confidently and joyously scatters seed in the furrows does the nourishing strength of the soil make itself freely available." Jewish scholarship, reared in the school of adversity and hence too little spoiled, was, he insisted, ready to make itself available to all who would learn. But while "it's rations are kept short and he who has so much to learn has no hesitancy to mount the teacher's chair, it would be unworthy and hypocritical to express gratitude."[3]

A quarter of a century earlier in 1871, Moritz Steinschneider, pinning his hopes for Jewish scholarship on its incorporation into the university, had curtly refused a position on the faculty of the Hochschule für Wissenschaft des Judentums; and in 1875, when the first report of the Hochschule was published, he recorded its appearance with some caustic remarks about "the new ghetto for Jewish learning." In 1876, he again refused an offer, this time from the Seminary in Budapest. "The subjects which he could teach," wrote Alexander Marx of the episode, "and his conception of Jewish scholarship would not fit an institution which held itself aloof from the university. He objected to special institutions for the training of rabbis and claimed that they nowadays promoted systematic hypocrisy and scholarly immaturity. What is scientific in Jewish history and literature does not fight shy of the universities and should be made available to Christians." His solution was the establishment of foundations supporting *Privatdozenten* in Jewish studies in the universities "in order to induce the government to establish professorships."

Marx noted apologetically Steinschneider's "one-sided and prejudiced attitude towards the Seminaries," and as well "his optimism regarding the possibilities of creating a place for Jewish learning at German universities, as had happened in England and America."[4] The "prejudice" is clearly evident; what the reasons for the optimism were are not so easily discerned. Yet he may have been partially correct. Perhaps the presence of *Privatdozenten* in Jewish studies could have forced the government's hand; but we shall never know.

What may have prompted Steinschneider's optimism was a very small straw in the wind, the appointment of Schiller-Szinessy as reader in rabbinics in Cambridge in 1866, followed almost two decades later by the appointment to a similar post, in Oxford, of Neubauer. On the American scene nothing comparable had happened to have encouraged Steinschneider. Jewish studies had not made their real entry into American universities at that time. William Rosenau, writing in 1896, a year after Kaufmann, on "Semitic Studies in American Universities" helps to illuminate the situation. While Hebrew had been an integral part of Harvard's curriculum from the time of its foundation and Lightfoot's library had been bequeathed to the College, only to be destroyed in the fire of 1764, the end of the eighteenth century had seen a decline of interest, so that in 1787 the then Professor of Oriental Languages surrendered the post to become Professor of English Grammar and Rhetoric. The last vestige of interest, until more recent times, was the Hebrew oration delivered at Commencement until 1817.

Without looking further at the details of Rosenau's survey, it is nonetheless interesting to observe his perspective. "An institution worthy of the title 'university,'" he wrote, "should have a chair in Semitics. It is recognized as one of the principle disciplines of all European Universities." How different is this from Kaufmann's recognition that Semitic studies, as carried out in European universities, were by no means an unmixed blessing if they could be considered a blessing at all vis-à-vis Jewish studies. The benefits accruing from the study of Semitics were, according to Rosenau, manifold, although none of those he mentioned related to Jewish literature or Judaism. However, he reported one delightful anecdote that is worthy of citation. "A student studying Political Economy at one of our colleges came to the Oriental seminary and asked to be enrolled. Said the professor to the student, 'What do you want with Semitics?' The answer was given: 'Well, my father told me that if I want to get a little common sense, I ought to take up a little Semitics.'"[5] I leave it to the specialists in oral tradition and form-criticism to reconstruct the father's original remark.

The intent of this historical investigation may not be entirely evident, yet it may provide some help in considering the present situation. There is no need to repeat, at this point, Arnold J. Band's report on "Jewish Studies in American Liberal Arts Colleges and Universities."[6] Nor is there need to recapitulate the ways in which, generally speaking, Jewish studies have been eased or nudged their way into the American universities. Jacob Neusner has done that in his paper, "Studies in Judaism: Modes and Contexts."[7] There he has made a most careful attempt to define Jewish studies and to distinguish the impact made by the auspices under or the setting in which they are undertaken. Neither is a response to this valuable inquiry and analysis here required. Yet in a sense the remainder of this paper reflects an uneasiness with its apparent readiness to acquiesce to the present structures imposed upon the field.

If my own academic career as a teacher of Jewish studies has taught me anything, it is the danger of the distortion of that field, of that tradition when external distinctions are imposed. I do not mean here to suggest a rejection of the methodology or methodologies of the humanistic disciplines among which I for one include history, but merely to warn that a distinction must be made between the methods and their results. It has been my experience that all too often the *structures* emerging from the application of the method to a particular area, *i.e.,* the results, are imposed upon another area without any opportunity being given to discover whether the method, if applied to a second body of material— without regard to the results in the first instance—may not yield an entirely different *structure.* A cogent example, it seems to me, is the structure of George Foot Moore's monumental study of Judaism. In a sense, the basic difference between that work and F. Weber's *System der Altsynagogalen Palästinenischen Theologie,* beyond the mastery of the subject by Moore as contrasted to Weber's derivative scholarship, is the *attitude*—the one negative, prompted by Lutheran piety, the other positive, controlled by liberal American Protestant ideas. Both, however, have no hesitancy whatsoever in applying the results of the Protestant theological method, *viz.,* the theological headings and terminology, the systematic structures that have emerged from an examination of that religious tradition, upon another content, Judaism.

Enlarging this now to the present problem: the imposition of structures derived from the particular and peculiar history of the American university upon new areas now being admitted to the groves of academe. An earlier example of this is to be found in the use Kaufmann made, in the article quoted above, of the term "Jewish theology" in his phrase, "the demand that Jewish theology be incorporated as a faculty of the university." It was the language he was forced to use, for Jewish studies broadly defined had no place within the traditional structure of the philosophical faculty nor of the Christian theological faculty. The only way they could have functioned as an integral unit, not as an ancillary to some other interest, would have been under the guise of a theological faculty, just as the Jewish community of the time had to function under the guise of an ecclesiastic institution—a church.

What is being said at this juncture is simply that the dismantling of Jewish learning as a totality, part being given over to religious studies, another to Near Eastern history and languages, a third to Germanic studies, etc., etc., so that it may be eased into the existing structures of the already fading, if not decaying, institutions of the American university is to sacrifice the future to immediate advantages. Indeed, I suggest that beyond and beneath the fustian and rhetoric of the blacks' demand for black studies is just such an awareness of this reality.

I cannot argue with Neusner's analysis and his definitions. They are impeccable and they do describe the scene; but they may turn out to be irrelevant. To acquiesce in the ideology that rationalizes the often indefensible structures of the American university is to join an army in retreat. If this brief historical survey can be said to have demonstrated anything it is that, in the past, the universities, in large measure, rejected Jewish studies because they recognized consciously or unconsciously that the field overrode their rubrics. If today unwillingness has been replaced by eagerness—indeed overeagerness—it may be simply because Jewish studies or their proponents have become ready to perform the kinds of mutilations and self-immolations that present-day university administrations and faculty educational-policy committees with their often unspoken, but nonetheless very real, ideologies require. What ought to concern us now, therefore, is not the role or roles Judaica has been playing in the present university, but how it can find a place in the emerging universities of tomorrow.

Students, I find, are concerned to be confronted by a Gestalt—a wholeness of form and matter. They are weary of the *disjecta membra* that have become the academic game. Jewish studies in their comparative newness in the American university have not yet undergone the ultimate atomization other disciplines have suffered. How to avoid this and to construct a viable process of Jewish studies, this I submit is the crucial question that may indeed try our souls.

NOTES

1. Leopold Zunz, *Gesammelte Schriften*, I, 41–59, "Die jüdische Literatur." For a critique of the approach to Judaism and its literature in the period see George Foot Moore, "Christian Writers on Judaism" in *Harvard Theological Review*, Vol. 14, (1921).

2. I discern an ironic word-play in *Vertretung*, for it means both representation and substitution.

3. *Monatschrift für Geschichte und Wissenschaft des Judentums*, (n.s. III), Vol. 39, pp. 145–167.

4. Alexander Marx, "Moritz Steinschneider" in *Essays in Jewish Biography* (Philadelphia, 1947), pp. 144–145.

5. *Yearbook of the Central Conference of American Rabbis*, Vol. VI (1897) pp. 99 *et seq.*

6. *American Jewish Yearbook*, Vol. 67 (1966), pp. 3–30.

7. *Journal of the American Academy of Religion*, XXXVII, 2 (June, 1969), pp. 131–140.

GRADUATE EDUCATION IN JUDAICA: PROBLEMS AND PROSPECTS

JACOB NEUSNER
Brown University
Professor of Religious Studies
and Head of the Graduate Program in
History of Religions: Judaism

I

EDUCATORS responsible for graduate programs, whatever the discipline or field, share a number of problems in common in defining their task and carrying it out.[1] While I shall concentrate on one aspect of a relatively modest field, namely graduate education in the study of Judaism in the context of the science of religion, I hope these concrete observations may contribute to a more general insight into the current situation.

First, however, comes the problem facing everyone: the demand for relevance. In the study of Judaism, as elsewhere, graduate students tell us their studies need to be relevant, though they are not often clear what they should be relevant *to*. Indeed, relevance means pretty much what you want it to mean: rejection of discipline in favor of subjectivity; the expectation of immediate achievement and instant wisdom; the assertion of egalitarianism in place of the aristocracy of knowledge; the imposition of opinion in place of, indeed in preference to, fact. Guided by mere impressions, we suppose everything is new. I suspect that the resentment voiced in the demands for "relevance" is far older than its new vocabulary. It represents a reaction to the age-old demands of rigorous scholarship. What, after all, does scholarship require, if not discipline, patience, respect for the knowledge and insight of others, suspicion of generalization, and reverence for facts? The existential realities actually have not changed much. We demand, first of all from ourselves, and also from our students, hard, sustained work, critical thought, and above all, mature judgment. But how many in any generation are capable of these attainments? We expect severe, if pointed and impersonal, criticism, rational commitment to disciplined learning, abdication of self in favor of truth, and submission of opinion to the court of learning. How many, in any

19

age, have had the maturity of character and the dedication to learning to endure these rewarding trials?

Scholarship is a function of character and personality as much as it is a product of memory, learning, patience, and hard work. A daring and courageous person will create daring and courageous theses. A patient and devoted mind will produce immaculate and abiding results. A constructive and amiable master will raise up self-confident disciples for the coming generation. Those lacking in confidence or intelligence will always be available to destroy and denigrate the best efforts of mature men. Above all, a critical and discerning intellect will invariably serve to purify and elevate the ideas of easily satisfied careerists.

We cannot define a Judaica Ph.D. out of context. In general, the Ph.D. represents as much variety as the universities that grant it and the scholars that take it. In my view, the Ph.D. marks a stage in one's development. It serves as a professional degree, not as the certification of virtue or of a perfected and completed, thus ended, education. The function of the Ph.D. program therefore needs to be carefully spelled out in the context of specific settings. In general such a program should educate men capable of continuing their own education and supervising that of others, able to pursue consequential inquiries in specific disciplines. The Ph.D. degree, as distinguished from the function of programs leading to it, obviously serves to certify college teachers—but what it certifies *about* them is that they have satisfactorily completed a program. True, the degree (apart from the program) serves other purposes, but these do not require specification here. When asked, "What must a person be able to be considered normal?" Freud replied, "Lieben und arbeiten," to love and to work. What must a person be able to *do* when he has completed a Ph.D. program and holds the degree? He must be able to read critically, to write accurately, to teach cogently, and to advance knowledge. Many are thus qualified, though not all who are granted the title deserve it.

II

Let me stress at the outset that while my assigned topic is *Graduate Education in Judaica,* I can deal with only a small aspect of it, and that is, graduate education in Judaica in the context of the study of religions. Again, I shall draw upon my very limited experience. I received my degree in one of the three programs in which Judaica is studied in the context of religious studies, at Columbia, and am making an effort to begin a second such program, at Brown. The data I shall mention are intended as exemplifications taken from a single, very limited situation.

Graduate education in Judaica presently flourishes in several other sorts of settings, including Departments of History, Near Eastern Languages and Literatures, and Departments of Jewish Studies. These programs serve different purposes; they draw upon different sorts of students, aim at different goals, and address themselves to a different constituency from mine. Each setting requires discussion in its own right. Nor should we ignore the fact that graduate studies in Judaica are undertaken in Jewish schools, both for the preparation of rabbis and teachers, and for the education of scholars in doctoral programs. That context is, again, quite separate from the several sorts of university departmental programs.

I stress, also, that studies of Judaica in departments of religion are not the only kinds of Judaic scholarship; Judaica cannot and ought not to be reduced to the study of the religion of the Jews. I am not persuaded that the best setting for Judaic studies is a department of religion, and I do not come to plead any such notion. Indeed, I should be the first to argue the contrary. Each discipline has its advantages; each field will make its contribution to the understanding of the whole.

While graduate education in the USA is a rather new phenomenon—the first graduate schools were founded at Harvard in 1872 and Johns Hopkins in 1876, less than a century ago—both undergraduate and graduate studies in the field of Judaica are even more recent. Aspects of Judaic studies—that is, "the discipline which deals with the historical experiences, in the intellectual, religious, and social spheres of the Jewish people in all centuries and countries"[2]—aspects of these studies were touched upon from earliest times. The study of the Hebrew language and Hebrew Scriptures is not new to American higher education, though the context was not Judaica. Today, moreover, aspects of Judaica are pursued in many disciplines of the social sciences and the humanities. Professors of Anthropology, Sociology, Psychology, not to mention Politics, Philosophy, History, Comparative Literature, Near Eastern Studies, History of Science—all make considerable contributions to Judaic learning.

Likewise, graduate programs in some phase of Judaic studies leading to the Ph.D. are available at Brandeis, Berkeley, Brown, UCLA, Chicago, Columbia, Cornell, Dropsie, Harvard, Indiana, Iowa, Johns Hopkins, Michigan, New York University, Hunter, Pennsylvania, Princeton, Rutgers, Smith, Temple, Texas, Vanderbilt, Wayne, Wisconsin at Madison, and Yale,[3] not to mention the many schools, including the above, which also offer Ph.D.'s in the study of the Bible. Many of these programs focus upon Hebrew language and literature in the context of Semitics or

Near Eastern studies in ancient, medieval, and modern times. Only a few concentrate on aspects of the history, religion, and culture of the Jews.

The picture is still more complicated by the development of various sorts of doctoral programs, apart from studies leading to rabbinical ordination, in Jewish schools, including Hebrew Union College, Jewish Theological Seminary and Yeshiva University. Colleges training teachers for the Jewish schools likewise grant doctorates.

The proliferation of all these kinds of programs is indeed, a new phenomenon. Arnold Band points out that eighty percent of the professors of Judaica in U.S. colleges and universities received their graduate training in the United States; of these, Columbia, through Salo Baron, and Harvard, through Harry Wolfson, have made by far the largest contribution.[4] Baron and Wolfson retired in very recent years, and the development of professional doctoral studies in Judaica cannot be dated much before their careers. Hence, the history of doctoral education in Judaica in the USA and Canada covers not more than half a century; more accurately, that history is approximately one generation old.

Definition of the field has barely begun. As Band observes, "It is almost impossible to tell what a man's specialty is unless one reads his publications or his doctoral thesis. The various areas of Jewish scholarship are so often undefined and interrelated that the terms used in academic titles or catalogue descriptions do not convey an exact meaning."[5] That is to say, the field is so primitive that the processes of definition, differentiation, and specialization are still incomplete.

As to the study of Judaism in the science of religion, doctoral programs in Judaica in departments of religious studies are located in Columbia, Temple, and Brown Universities. The former is well established; the latter two began last year. In addition, graduate study of Judaism is carried on in the Department of Near Eastern and Judaic Studies at Brandeis University, in various departments and programs at Yeshiva University, Jewish Theological Seminary, Dropsie College, and a few other places. Graduates of such programs, however, rarely have the opportunity to take courses in the study of religions. Approaching the teaching of Judaism in undergraduate programs, they suppose the primary requirement is "objectivity"! They have slight, if any, notion of what their colleagues do, and why. If, therefore, the function of a Ph.D. is to prepare college teachers for various departments, then with the increase of Judaica positions in departments of religious studies, doctoral programs located in graduate departments in *that* particular field will have to assume much of the burden of preparing qualified Judaica teachers.

III

Graduation education in Judaica in a department of religious studies aims at preparing teachers of Judaica *for such departments*. I must underline this modest intention. Clearly, only a part of the phenomena of Judaic studies finds a place in the study of religions. When the disciplines of history of religions and theology, religious ethics, textual and literary criticism, social scientific studies of religions and philosophy of religion —that is, the disciplines normally present among the faculty of a department of religious studies—come to bear upon Judaic data, scholars in such disciplines naturally select among the varieties of data those aspects best studied through their methods. Further, the phenomena of Judaism, like those derived from other religious traditions, in this context are not self-validating, of interest "for their own sake." They are important because they exemplify something of interest to the historian of religion, the theologian, the social scientist, and to the philosopher of religion. One may criticize the method and results of these disciplines, but so far as the method is sound for any data, it is acceptable for Judaic ones as well.

Graduate Judaic education in a department of religious studies, therefore, should equip the young scholar with a method, or better still, a variety of methods, inquiries, and issues, which he may bring to bear upon the study of Judaism. The graduate student, furthermore, ought to have some insight into the way in which these methods work elsewhere, on other sorts of material or on other religious traditions. And he should have some considerable familiarity with the history of the study of religions, with the "theory of religion," and comparative data. He should work both as an expert in comparative religious studies concentrating on one body of data and as a master of a variety of methods of research, applying these to Judaism studies. The young doctor ought, moreover, to have a broad grasp of Judaism, so that he can teach a variety of courses and, in his scholarly work, cite data from more than one country, period, or genre of literature. If his subject is religion, and within it, Judaism, he should be able either to make general observations on religion and on Judaism, or—a more reasonable requirement—to recognize the limitations of such observations.

He requires, furthermore, a particular scholarly field or problem. He needs to stand within a tradition of Judaic learning. Within the field of religious studies, one such tradition is the study of Jewish mysticism, created by Gershom Scholem. Another is the study of Jewish philosophy, developed by Harry A. Wolfson. Others, are the studies of particular periods and documents, or archaeological data, such as the religion of

Israel in ancient times, or the nature of Judaism in late antiquity as revealed in talmudic and archaeological materials. Models for the tradition of the study of religions in late antiquity are the late Arthur Darby Nock and my teacher Morton Smith. The tradition of textual commentary, so deeply rooted in the history of Judaism, has in recent times been enhanced by the application of the philological and form-critical methods. I may point to Saul Lieberman and the late Y. N. Epstein as noteworthy masters of the philological method. Form-criticism and source criticism of Judaic literature are represented by Abraham Weiss, Joseph Heinemann, and David Weiss, among the currently active generation. I offer these few instances to clarify what I mean by a "tradition" within a particular scholarly field.

My own ambition is to advance the historical study of talmudic and cognate literature in the context of the histories of the Jews and Judaism, and of the history of religions in late antiquity. The two Talmuds have long been studied by lawyers and philologists, so we have the advantage of an immense corpus of scholarship, both traditional and modern. The study of Talmudic and other Judaism of the period in which the Talmuds were created, and to which they testify, is still incomplete. We have, for example, no corpus of biographies of the great rabbis. We have no systematic accounts of the character of various rabbinical schools. We have few sophisticated and comparative studies of the theological and other religious concepts of the rabbinical movement, or of particular authorities and generations. It is no criticism of the work of Louis Ginzberg, Schechter and Moore, Marmorstein, Büchler, and Isaac Hirsch Weiss, Graetz, Yawitz and Halevy, Aaron Hyman and Y. S. Zuri, E. R. Goodenough, and, among the living, Abraham J. Heschel, Salo Baron, Samuel Belkin and E. E. Urbach—the list is not much longer—to observe that much remains to be done.

I believe that the study of rabbinical literature from late antiquity as well as of pertinent materials from other sources can be fruitfully pursued in departments of religious studies. True, not everything worthwhile in these data will be exhausted by scholarship under such auspices. Careful commentary on texts, translations, philological and related studies will always find worthwhile tasks. These problems are apt to be solved best through disciplines other than those of religious studies, in departments of Semitics and Near Eastern languages, for one example, or in Jewish rabbinical seminaries, for another. But the study of rabbinic Judaism cannot fail to be enriched by the context provided by the study of religions in general and of religions in late antiquity in particular.

IV

It is easier to make these demands than to meet them. When we come to the planning of particular programs of studies, the difficulties become acute. Moreover, each school must to some extent try to meet them in its own way, which will be determined to a large extent by its particular advantages and limitations. Here, accordingly, I do not think we can lay down general rules. Let me report merely what we have been trying to do in shaping the new graduate program in History of Religions: Judaism, at Brown. In line with what has already been said, our purpose is clear: to educate young scholars as teachers of Judaica in departments of religious studies, to enhance their knowledge both of pertinent, related religious traditions and of the study of religions; to set them on scholarly projects in a particular tradition and concerning a particular body of data in a circumscribed place and period in the history of Judaism. Concentrating our best energies on this modest project, we hope to make a solid, if limited, contribution to Judaica.

The success, if any, with which our purposes are achieved is measured in two sets of examinations. The first, at the end of a year of study, concentrates on the comparative aspect, and consists of papers in theory of religion, early Christianity, and theology. The second, preliminary to the dissertation, covers in varying ways the four conventional periods of the history of Judaism: biblical, talmudic, medieval, and modern. The papers concentrate on scholarly traditions, rather than on the reading of texts drawn from these periods. Students need to know the chief scholarly issues, the important scientific works, the central themes of the several periods. A further examination focuses upon preparation for the dissertation itself. The result ought to be broad knowledge of the field as a scholarly enterprise and, also, access to scholarship in cognate fields.

What advantages do we enjoy? These, I think, are not ours alone. First, while the preliminary preparation in languages and texts is necessarily considerable, schools and programs in Hebrew language and literature abound in this country. The level is not invariably high; but we can realistically decline admission to beginners in the Hebrew language and in rabbinic literature. We are able to set as a standard for admission some familiarity with rabbinic documents.

Furthermore, we are fortunate enough to be located near other universities offering complementary studies. Our graduate students may pursue readings in medieval Judaism, for example, in consultation with Professor Alexander Altmann at Brandeis University. We are able to invite specialists in fields not represented on our modest faculty to serve as examiners, on dissertation committees, and as counselors. Indeed, we are able to attempt to specialize precisely because substantial scholarly resources are nearby. In time to come, I hope a consortium may take shape so that students in the field of Judaica, registered in one graduate program, may take courses or even enroll for an entire semester or year of study at other graduate schools offering subjects unavailable at home. If today there is no "one place" for the study of Judaica, that disability represents a splendid opportunity for each university to develop its particular interests and areas of specialization. Through cooperative arrangements, both formal and informal, we shall be able to turn the limitations of each university into advantages for the field as a whole.

We all benefit from the elaborate Judaica programs of Jewish seminaries and other institutions of higher Jewish learning. Students may qualify for admission by acquiring elsewhere the rudiments of method along with the necessary language skills and experience in reading texts before embarking on graduate work in our department. We are not equipped to teach these fundamental skills, but we must demand them. A college student aspiring to devote himself to Judaic studies today may begin work, not in a graduate program such as the ones I have described, but in an institution of higher Jewish learning in the USA or the State of Israel. A "general education in Judaic studies," equivalent to the achievements of a major in English after high-school and college years, may well be attained in a few years of study, for example, at the Hebrew University. I encourage students, where possible, to go first to Jerusalem for a year or two, then to Brown, then back to Jerusalem or to an equivalent program in this country for further study. They are thereby able to acquire the broad and comprehensive learning we are unable to provide. They bring to us the insights and perspectives of colleagues elsewhere. If few undergraduates are satisfactorily educated to undertake the kind of scholarship we envision, many opportunities exist to achieve the requisite breadth and depth.

V

Problems yet to be solved are of two classes. First are those presented by the cultural environment. In all aspects of Judaica, not only in the ones mentioned earlier, we have a superfluity of experts. Every Jew who has read a book or two—and some who have not—regards himself not merely as a primary datum in the history of Judaism, but also as a significant authority. Everyone's opinion carries preponderant weight, it seems, and in particular every rabbi knows it all. Both we and our students need to insulate ourselves from the appeal of omniscience. We must reenforce our commitment to specialization, therefore, to competence in some few things. We must present a contrast: even among the things we need to know, we do not claim to be everywhere expert, but gladly rely on others and submit to their judgment and criticism.

A further environmental problem is created by several related opinions: first, the belief that without mastery, or at least considerable study, of the Babylonian Talmud in the classical mode, no one can do anything of importance in the Judaic field; second, and related to this, is the view that study of the Talmud without much understanding is meritorious in itself; third, that study of the Talmud can be done effectively only by the method of the classical yeshiva; finally, that the experience of alienation from the yeshiva's standards and conversion to those of modern historical scholarship is necessary for scientific work in Judaism. These beliefs together constitute a formidable obstacle for young men who have grown up in other than traditional Jewish schools and yet aspire to contribute to Judaic studies. The first is obviously false for the pretalmudic period and, except in study of law and legal literature, probably false for the later periods as well. The second statement is its own refutation. The third, that study of the Talmud can be done only in a classical yeshiva, cannot be settled by an argument. Sooner or later someone will settle it by making himself a first-rate Talmudist without going to a yeshiva, perhaps by studying at the Hebrew University's excellent program as an alternative. I see no reason why it cannot be done. If one does not have to go to a yeshiva to master the Talmud, then it follows that one need not be alienated to acquire the attitude of historical scholarship. In any event, besides the religious belief in the necessity of yeshiva training, this position derives much of its support from the fact that so many great scholars of the past three or four generations followed this road. This was understandable, for there was then no thorough teaching of Talmud outside of yeshivas, so of course it could not be mastered elsewhere. But now things are different. Opportunities do exist.

This is an especially important fact because of the tasks which lie before us, tasks not yet completed by those who have conformed to the pattern held up to us, not only as a religious ideal, but as the exclusive means of preparation for Judaic scholarship. We do not have translations of the corpus of rabbinical literature into European languages. We do not have a complete, scientifically consistent philological commentary for the Babylonian Talmud. We have not got even an incomplete and modest commentary of any sort for the whole of the Palestinian Talmud, which

has never been properly translated. We do not yet have a complete con-
cordance of either Talmud, nor of the greater part of midrashic literature.
We do not even have critical texts for much of talmudic and cognate literature, nor even thorough compendia of variant readings for the whole
corpus. We do not have a decent dictionary for rabbinical literature of
late antiquity, certainly none providing up-to-date etymological studies.
We do not have a thorough, detailed introduction to talmudic literature,
one in which each document is carefully described and dated, and in
which the manuscript evidence is summarized and evaluated. We have
no history or comprehensive description of Talmudic law. These are the
sorts of work which could best have been undertaken by those made familiar with the sources by a classical education in a traditional talmudic
school. But with respect and gratitude for what has been achieved by
those who studied first in yeshivas, then in universities, I find no reason
for other sorts of students to be excluded or intimidated. Much remains
to be done, both by those with traditional and then critical, philological
training, and by those with entirely other kinds of education. One does
not have to denigrate the value of a particular educational pattern in
order to show the viability of some other one. But it will *not* do to insist
on education of one kind *only* for tasks which have not yet been achieved.

VI

Besides these problems, which are environmental and therefore beyond
easy solution—but not critical, merely lingering—there is another set of
difficulties which results from the novelty of Judaic studies in universities.
These can be solved, but they are critical. Let me list some which have
yet to be worked out.

First, we have no adequate source of fellowships, particularly for the
peripatetic students I described. Too few universities provide graduate
fellowships for foreign study, almost none have any for study in other
United States universities. There can be no consortium without fellowship support such as is now unavailable.

Second, we have no satisfactory system for placement or means of determining who is qualified for which position. A department of religion
may not be well served by a Semitist, a department of Near Eastern or
Oriental studies, by a historian of Judaism. The differentiation of programs and consequent placement procedures thus is still inadequate. Even
the practical ways by which candidates make themselves available and
positions are made known is haphazard. This is a problem that is faced
in many fields. In the area of the study of Judaism in religion depart-

ments it is likely to be solved by the new Council on the Study of Religion, organized under the auspices of the American Council of Learned Societies by several organizations of religion scholars.

Third, I am not persuaded that a sufficient number of positions exist for the growing number of prospective doctors. Growth in universities has slowed down, and new fields are competing for limited budgets. Since rabbinical seminaries generally prefer to employ their own doctors and in any event, quite correctly impose conditions of conviction and religious practice, those educated for university teaching and scholarship are not invariably qualified for Jewish institutional employment. Other posts cannot be taken for granted. We must avoid making false promises to young men and women considering careers in Judaica.

Fourth, we have not fully defined the range of scholarly tasks we can undertake and satisfactorily carry out. We have no curriculum or better still, set of curricula, appropriate to our field. The modest program I described earlier has yet to take shape in a rational set of courses, so that, in a few years, a person may learn all the things he needs to know to do his job as here defined. Some other programs in Judaica do not aspire to even this much coherence and cogency. Without differentiation or adequate specialization, Judaica is so defined that one may acquire a doctorate in the field on the basis of studies in scarcely related subjects, e.g., in biblical studies, medieval mysticism, and American Jewish history.

Fifth, we, above all, lack a context for our individual studies. We work as autodidacts, approaching problems successfully solved by others or, more commonly, ignoring mistakes made by others. Each new scholarly book and article should come as an event for celebration. We must rejoice in the achievements of colleagues, take pride in them, find hope in their accomplishment. Books and articles of considerable sophistication and originality—meticulous translations, intelligent, comprehensive, and critical studies—must these be read only by the authors' friends and students? Can we not see ourselves as a fellowship of learning men, strengthened by one another, concerned for one another? Separately, after all, we do not add up to much. Together, we constitute a grand collegium, as the French reviewers refer to us: "the American Jewish school." But if we are a school, where is our journal? Where do we find substantial and constructive, critical reviews of serious books? Where do we even meet one another? These problems do not confront Judaica alone, still less the study of the history of Judaism. They are part of the challenge facing graduate educators as a whole.[6]

VII

I shall close on a personal note. When I taught at Dartmouth, much as I enjoyed undergraduates, I thought, "If only I could teach graduate students, then . . . " Now at Brown I find undergraduate teaching a greater joy than ever, but graduate education looms up as an insurmountable mountain of difficulties, one obstacle more intimidating than the last. I find myself tempted to give up at the very outset, to concentrate solely on teaching undergraduates and perhaps graduates in other fields, and to pursue my own education and scholarly efforts. Perhaps in a little while I shall succumb to that temptation, but for the present I do not give up. The task, if difficult, is not unimportant. According to the effort is the reward. And, to quote R. Tarfon, to whom I devoted my earliest endeavors, "The work is not yours to complete. But you are not free to desist from it."*

NOTES

1. The best account of Judaic studies in United States universities is Arnold J. Band, "Jewish Studies in American Liberal Arts Colleges and Universities," *American Jewish Yearbook 1966,* Vol. 67 (Philadelphia and New York: 1966), Jewish Publication Society and American Jewish Committee, pp. 3–30; see also my "Judaica in the University: Modes and Contexts," in the George Thomas *Festschrift,* in press, Princeton University Press. I found few items of any depth or profundity on graduate study in general. Many surveys and compilations of data exist; I know of little with vitality or intelligence. Of some interest are Oliver C. Carmichael, *Graduate Education: A Critique and a Program* (N.Y.: 1961), Harper & Brothers, pp. 3–158; and Everett Walters, ed., *Graduate Education Today* (Washington: 1965), American Council on Education, pp. 1–29, 185–201.

2. Band, p. 5. See my "Judaism in the History of Religions," *History and Theory on Method in the History of Religions,* Beiheft VIII, pp. 32–34; and "Modes and Contexts of Judaic Studies," *Journal of the American Academy of Religion,* 37, 2, (June: 1969), pp. 131–140.

3. Band, p. 14. The list may be longer today.

4. Band, p. 15.

5. Band, p. 15.

6. My thanks to Professors Morton Smith, Wendell Dietrich, Ernest Frerichs, Gerald Blidstein, Avrum Udovitch, and Claude Welch, for helpful criticism.

* A slightly revised version of this paper served as my Presidential Address at the annual meeting of the American Academy of Religion, Boston, October 24, 1969, and was published in *Journal of the American Academy of Religion,* XXXVII, 4, 1969, pp. 321–330.

THE BIBLE AND JUDAIC STUDIES

NAHUM SARNA
Brandeis University
Golding Professor of Biblical Studies

EVER since Solomon Schechter characterized "Higher Biblical Criticism" as "higher anti-Semitism," this somewhat unfortunate *bon mot* has furnished an excuse for ignorance and mental inertia, and has served to obscure the very real and valid problems which biblical scholarship has raised. It has also had the effect of belittling the intellectual achievements, of no mean order, of those who devoted themselves to their solution. Worse still, it has somehow conveyed the impression that biblical studies are not quite *bon ton* and, in fact, like idolatry, constitute a sphere of human activity that the Almighty has reserved specifically for the non-Jews.

The title of this paper is an ominously discouraging example of such sentiment, hinting, as it does, that the Bible is not necessarily part of Judaic studies. Even more distressing is the oft-presented question as to whether there is a Jewish point of view to the Bible. The very formulation in this manner implies the possibility of disengagement by the Jew from his biblical heritage and suggests, absurdly, the ability objectively to measure the Scriptures by some yardstick that is clearly, definably, and characteristically "Jewish." It harbors the insinuation that such critical appraisal might, indeed, eventuate in a negative response to the query. To ask whether there is a Jewish point of view to the Talmud would quite properly be regarded as self-contradictory in nature and the apotheosis of frivolity. Yet the same question does not seem to be equally ludicrous in respect to the Bible.

Now this is a very strange phenomenon for, throughout the millenia of exile, the Hebrew Scriptures naturally occupied a central place in Jewish tradition; nay, they constituted its very protoplasm and the animating force of Jewish existence. The Bible *is* a Jewish point of view if only by virtue of its being the product of the Jewish people and of its having

35

been regarded as the most faithful witness to the national past, the primary
source for the knowledge and use of the national language, the font of
truth, wisdom, law, and morality for the people of Israel, the inspiration
for its life style and the embodiment of the hopes and dreams of a
glorious future. To repeat: the Bible *is* a Jewish point of view.

It will be noticed, I hope, that I have deliberately used the indefinite
pronoun, for the fact of the matter is that while the Hebrew Scriptures
constitute, indeed, the substructure of Jewish civilization, they are just
that. They represent the earliest, the formative stage of Jewish tradition
of which all subsequent layers are but the explication, amplification,
expansion and elaboration, and in which the Bible remains the active
metabolizing agent. Whatever may be thought of Max Weber's sociological analysis of biblical religion, he was certainly correct in referring
to the object of his study as "ancient Judaism" *(Das antike Judentum).*

For these reasons, it ought to be self-evident that no program of
Judaica studies in any university can do justice to the subject without
thorough investigation of the biblical foundations. Yet, *mirabile dictu,*
as far as I have been able to ascertain, this elementary and obvious
desideratum is generally quite conspicuously absent from the curriculum
of studies, or it rarely serves as the base upon which the superstructure
is erected.

This somewhat bizarre situation is admittedly complicated and derives
from a combination of powerful factors, some non-Jewish in origin, some
of the product of Jewish anxiety.

In the first place, a kind of gentlemen's agreement has long existed
that requires biblical studies in the universities to be a Christian monopoly. Its origin is historico-political in that so often the university developed out of a divinity school, and it is theological in that it issues from
the dogma that the Hebrew Scriptures are *praeparatio* and that Jewish
exegesis is, accordingly, a distortion of the "truth." I am not insinuating,
heaven forfend, that latter-day enlightened Christian scholars either subscribe to both these propositions or utilize them for discriminatory purposes. I am suggesting that a subconscious, residual, carry-over of a
particular piece of medieval Christian dogmatism does frequently prevent
Jewish university students from studying the Bible under Jewish auspices.

An equally influential factor in this type of cultural deprivation is to
be located in the Jewish sphere. The teaching of the Bible today,
especially in the universities, is widely regarded as a venture fraught with
incalculable, but decidedly deleterious consequences. One hesitates to pry
open the lid of a theological Pandora's box, for few teachers are confident

of being able to handle the concomitant ills. Jewish scholarship, even at this late date, has hardly come to grips, let alone terms, with its biblical dimension. The study of the Scriptures still remains the unfortunate stepchild of traditional Jewish learning. In any event, the effect of all this is that Jewish students receive their introduction to the Bible from non-Jewish theological ax-grinders or through one-sided, uninformed, literature courses, or they may go through their Judaic courses blissfully ignorant that the Bible is a Jewish production.

The sensitive core of the problem is, in my opinion, to be located in the role of the Western university in the twentieth century. Among the prime functions of a modern university education is the stimulation of intellectual curiosity, the instillation of a conviction that truth must prevail over tradition, that reason and not authority is the final arbiter of truth, and that research must be conducted with scholarly objectivity unhampered by doctrinal considerations and untempered by apologetics.

These ideals of a modern university represent a radical departure from its medieval counterpart which essentially constituted a repository of accumulated knowledge which it strove to transmit intact and more or less uncritically. Among the last living vestiges of this medieval approach is the present-day yeshivah institution, and it is no accident that biblical studies are completely neglected here. Nor is it accidental that the products of yeshivah schools, usually students of the highest scholastic attainments, avoid the area of biblical studies even if they participate in Judaics courses when they enter the universities. Those few who do try their hand usually find it an unhappy experience.

No better off are the products of our synagogue-affiliated afternoon schools. These unfortunates seem doomed to spend the most impressionable years of their lives acquiring a childish conception of the Bible teaching the university. By this we mean scholars whose training has Jewish scholarship, building on the achievements of their non-Jewish and, should one of them wander into a university course in this area, the motive is usually to gain a "cheap credit." For alas, these young men usually have the notion that the study of the Scriptures is not really a discipline. In short, no undergraduate seems to come as a *tabula rasa* in this field, but rather as a bearer of prejudices, misinformation, and spurious problems of faith. The net result is the need for a considerable amount of unlearning.

All this, it will be agreed, presents a series of problems not encountered in regard to the other areas of Judaic studies, and the situation is further complicated by the fact that the modern university, as defined above, must by its very nature exclude the evangelist. It is not the function of a professor to promote or resolve issues of faith. It is not the purpose of a Judaic studies program to cater to students who are seeking identity— and in this respect it has nothing in common, either ideologically or functionally, with the issue of "Black Studies." A Jewish student may, indeed, and frequently does, find identity and commitment to be the desirable by-products of his studies, but that is not an element that enters into the planning and execution of the curriculum. The latter has as its sole objective the scientific exploration of all facets of the civilization of the Jewish people, its properties and products, within the wider context of the university's educational structure, free from the taint of *odium theologicum*.

Does this mean, then, that the instructor has to be completely insensitive to the effects of his teaching, totally oblivious of the problems of an emotional, intellectual, and religious nature raised for the undergraduate by the sudden confrontation with new perspectives and a critical approach? Must one suppress this sensitivity because one functions within the scope of a university structure? On the other hand, must the demonstration of sensibility inevitably involve the sacrifice of intellectual honesty and the compromise of academic integrity?

It seems to me that the primary goal in Bible teaching is neither to defend nor to criticize, but to understand the material better by drawing upon all the manifold resources that modern scholarship has placed at our disposal. By utilizing the material remains of the past, the accepted methods of historical research, the sciences of palaeography and linguistics, Semitic languages and literatures, comparative religion and a host of allied studies, Bible teaching is removed from its intellectual isolation and brought into correlation with the wider university curriculum. The more successful the attempt, the greater the repute gained for the subject as a respectable discipline.

The next stage of teaching engages the student in the place of the Bible in the context of the ancient world. It involves the exploration of the thought processes and modes of literary expression common to the Near East, and it should issue in the important lesson that truth is not necessarily coincident with "historical fact," and that literalism may, more often than not, be its deadly enemy. The imaginative and pictorial thinking of biblical man found expression in the concrete, the emotional, the poetic. To get behind the written word, one has to disengage the idea from the idiom, separate the metaphor from the reality behind it.

In this connection, it is thoroughly legitimate within the framework of a Judaic studies program to invoke the cardinal rabbinic principle of the multiple sense of Scripture. Judaism has no monolithic, logically self-consistent "orthodox" system of biblical exegesis, as anyone who can read the rabbinic Bible ought to know. The talmudic interpretation of Jer. 23: 29, as formulated in B. Sanh. 34ᵃ, found expression not only in the multiplicity of exegesis, but also in the remarkable ability harmoniously to encompass within a single tradition the most diverse approaches, which are frequently mutually exclusive.

It goes without saying, but it warrants repetition, that biblical studies have to constitute an intellectual challenge to be negotiated with intellectual honesty. There must be no repression of facts or issues, no un-problems. At the same time, it cannot be too strongly emphasized that a "scientific" or "critical" approach is not to be construed as an iconoclastic one for then the whole educational enterprise becomes self-defeating.

The history of Jewish exegesis is replete with critical observations ranging from textual to historical problems. In fact, there is hardly an issue, in what is today known as "lower" and "higher" criticism, to which the rabbinic and medieval exegetes did not respond in the light of their own presuppositions and with the limited tools available to them. We do not have the right to assume, disrespectfully, that had these authorities lived today, and had they access to modern knowledge and critical methodology, that they would have willfully and blindly rejected our solutions. It must be admitted, though, that the idea of the heterogeneous composition of the Pentateuch might be an exception to his statement. In the university, however, the issue is solely a scholarly one with the facts allowed to speak for themselves. I, for one, do not regard these problems as belonging to the realm of faith, piety, reverence, or spirituality. Those to whom modern categories are natural, and who have no need to un-learn, or who have successfully completed the unlearning process, will encounter a richer and altogether ennobling appreciation of Scripture. For those who insist on elevating a problem of psychology into one of faith, it can be observed that God can as effectively work through four documents as through one and that He can as well unfold His revelation in successive stages as in a single moment of time.

Still, it must never be lost sight of that, as early as one can trace, the Jewish people did not exhibit any awareness of source differentiation. The impact of the Bible upon it was as an integrated whole, as an entity complete in itself. Hence, it is inadequate to teach the Scriptures solely as a conglomerate of sources, as the sum total of its component elements. Like the merging of tastes or odors, or like the harmony and blending of musical notes, the constituents of biblical literature surely become, in combination, something quite new that contains qualities and properties not present in them as they exist in isolation.

For this reason, the main focus of biblical study at the undergraduate level should be the world-views of the writers, their ideas about God, man, and society, their profound sense of human destiny—all this in comparison and in contrast with the world-views of their Near Eastern contemporaries. It is here, after all, in the realm of ideas and values, that the Bible exerted its influence upon the Jewish people and the world. By placing the emphasis in this area of study, the transition is natural to the early rabbinic period, the next stage in the development of Jewish civilization.

BIBLICAL STUDIES IN JEWISH PERSPECTIVE

WILLIAM HALLO
Yale University
Professor of Assyriology
and Curator of the Babylonian Collection,
Yale University

T HE proposed title of our discussion[1] is thoroughly ambiguous. I have had to subject it to a certain amount of exegesis to try to recover its proper meaning. If the question means, Is there *a* Jewish point of view in Biblical Studies, i.e. one single, authoritative, agreed upon point of view in the sense that there is, or perhaps once was, a Catholic point of view, the answer must obviously be no. If we could really say: "take now your point of view, your only one, the one that you love," it would be only right to continue, "and sacrifice it on the nearest mountain." It has often been said that there are as many Jewish points of view on any issue as there are Jews, and this needs to be qualified for our views on Biblical Studies only by the sad fact that so many of our fellow Jews would have to plead "no opinion" on this particular issue. That still leaves at least as many Jewish viewpoints on Biblical Studies as there are Jewish Biblicists.

And so we pass on to another possible reading of the question: Do Biblical Studies belong in a Judaica curriculum or should the Jewish dimension, the Jewish administration if you like, of that curriculum be confined to post-Biblical Judaism? The question practically answers itself. In a day and age when black students are demanding black teachers for black studies; when a respected Islamicist urges his colleagues to publish in Arabic,[2] it hardly needs stressing that the Bible, as *the* fountainhead of Jewish thought and experience, cannot be excluded from Judaica programs. I would not go so far as to deny the right of our secular universities also to offer general courses on the Bible as literature, or the Bible in art, or even the Bible as a source-book for Christian doctrine. I am not even prepared to grant that this "right" has been abused in the past, that Biblical Studies are, or have been, a Christian monopoly at American universities. But we are not here to argue statistics. If Biblical Studies were a Christian field in this sense, then it would follow that biology was a Jewish one—or Assyriology for that matter. (Maybe that's why I was asked to ponder the question!) Yet we don't look for a Jewish point of view in biology, or even in Assyriology. We can be fairly

43

objective in these fields—or rather our particular subjectivity is colored by factors other than our religion. The same would be true of Qumran studies where it is surely too early for "a Jewish point of view" or even *any* "Jewish point of view" to have emerged. Similarly for the whole inter-testamental field, let alone the New Testament, though Samuel Sandmel has given us one interesting "Jewish *understanding* of the new Testament."

Of course on any reading, the question before us concerns itself with the Hebrew Bible alone, to the exclusion of Apocrypha and certainly of the New Testament. But this very limitation already implies one very definitely Jewish approach to the subject. And it is a limitation which involves a goodly number of others—for example typology (in the sense favored by our Christian colleagues), and more importantly theology as a whole. Now it is true that many Christian scholars would also like to see theology and exegesis kept strictly apart in Biblical Studies. A memorable plea to this effect was made by Will Irwin when he summed up the state of the field in a presidential address to the Society of Biblical Literature a decade ago. "Is there, or should there be *any* difference between Jewish and Christian exegesis?" he asked and concluded that, provided theology were kept at bay "In its central part . . . there will be and can be no distinction between Jewish and Christian exegesis."[3]

But I am not so sure that this answer remains valid today. I am not as confident as he was that the disciplines of hermeneutics and homiletics can be separated; that scholars of different and mutually exclusive persuasion can join together in an objective determination of the original meaning of the Biblical text, only to part company when studying the meanings that have subsequently been read into it, or when putting it to their own uses themselves. I am not even sure that we can be truly objective and impartial in determining the original text. I submit, rather, that Christian and Jewish points of view already part company precisely at this more basic level, i.e., in their respective attitudes toward the text.

The fence which Rabbinical tradition built around the law was really a fence around *the words* of the law, around the text.[4] I am not alone in thinking that much of Rabbinical exegesis, halakhic and especially aggadic, was inspired less by the desire to elucidate the text than by the need to protect and to fix it—in the mind and in the life of the people. Granted that an occasional Midrash relied on an inferior reading, or even a conscious emendation (signaled by *al tigrē . . . ellā*), on the whole the system worked. Critics may argue whether the meter of Ps. 29 can best be salvaged by adding or excising a verse, but either course would spoil the point of the Midrash that links its eighteen mentions of the Tetragrammaton with the eighteen benedictions of the Amidah.

Nor was Rabbinical exegesis the only inherently Jewish means of fixing the text. Liturgical use of the original Hebrew impressed the traditional readings indelibly on each new generation, and we can only chuckle at the story that when Heinrich Graetz served as $ba^c al$ $q\bar{o}r\bar{e}$, he recited a text emended according to his own scholarly tastes. Beyond Midrash and liturgy of course, the Masoretes made the text their main concern. But perhaps the most effective guarantee of textual fidelity was the traditional pride of place which the original text has always had over any translation in Jewish life. Translations have, it is true, existed wherever and whenever Hebrew dropped to the status of second language (or worse) among the Jews. But these translations never displaced the original Hebrew as they did in the Church. On the contrary, they served an important secondary function besides simple translation: in many instances they interpreted or reinterpreted the text, adjusting its original meaning to the theological requirements or tastes of a newer age. By thus providing an outlet for semantic change (e.g., the suppression of anthropomorphisms in various Targumim), they removed one major motive for violating the original text.

I would submit, then, that the living and continuous tradition of post-Biblical Judaism has, by these and other means, preserved a text that is essentially reliable, even while allowing each new generation to read new meanings into it. And while I cannot demonstrate the same for the prehistory of the canonical text, neither have I seen it disproved with solid evidence. A contrary point of view has been argued with eloquence by a distinguished member of this audience, who holds that, in a living tradition, meaning remains inviolate, even at the cost of textual corruption and modernization. As a result, he condones emendation by the modern scholar to a much larger extent than I would.[5] At the risk of being labeled pseudorthodox, I suggest that this difference between viewpoints is significant of a wide and potentially constructive difference of opinion; that the Jewish scholar, or rather the scholar approaching the Hebrew Bible in the context of a living Jewish tradition for which his personal Judaism is neither a sine qua non nor a universal guarantee, respects the *text* as a largely inviolate heritage fixed by millennia of Rabbinical exegesis, liturgical recitation, and Masoretic statistics; but that he can search for its original meaning without let or hindrance, knowing that its *meaning* within his tradition has always been subject to change. Here, then, is *a* Jewish point of view whose creative contribution should be available to Bible students of whatever persuasion.

NOTES

1. The following remarks were prepared as a response to Professor Sarna's original presentation. They are here reproduced, with minor changes, as an independent contribution.

2. J. Stetkevych, *Journal of Near Eastern Studies* 28 (1969) 145ff.

3. *Journal of Biblical Literature* 78 (1959) 8, 10.

4. Judah Goldin, *Harvard Theological Review* 58 (1965) 365 ff.

5. Morton Smith, *Journal of Biblical Literature* 88 (1969) 24.

ON THE TEACHING OF TALMUD IN
THE AMERICAN UNIVERSITY

BARUCH A. LEVINE
New York University
Professor of Hebrew

IT is my purpose, in the remarks which follow, to advocate the introduction of the systematic teaching of Talmud into the curriculum of the American university, where it is now relatively neglected. This proposal is set forth on the strength of seven years of experience in teaching Talmud at Brandeis University, from 1961 to 1968. I would like, first of all, to report on this effort and to evaluate its results.

Each year, a semester course of three hours of classroom instruction was offered in the Babylonian Talmud; a reading course was sometimes available during the alternate semester. The text of the Talmud was studied consecutively. Participants were not required to present prior experience in Talmud study, but a sound knowledge of Hebrew was necessary. Some of the students who enrolled in these courses over the years had studied Talmud previously at yeshiva-sponsored high schools, at more advanced yeshivot, at Hebrew Teachers' Colleges and their high schools, at the various schools of the Jewish Theological Seminary and the Ramah camps, and even at the Hebrew University. The classes ranged in size from six to fifteen. Because of personnel limitations, graduates and undergraduates studied together, but assignments were scaled appropriately. Hebrew was the language of instruction except when, as on one occasion, it had to be sacrificed so as to allow for the participation of a Christian graduate student who did not have command of modern spoken Hebrew.

Several specific objectives motivated most of the students who enrolled. Some undergraduates were preparing for entry into Rabbinical seminaries. Graduate students in modern Hebrew literature were encouraged to study Talmud so as to become somewhat familiar with its literary forms and idiom.

I was not able during these years to train graduate students for

advanced work in the Talmud, and the best that can be said is that, over
the years, several students got their start in Talmud at Brandeis and went
on to further studies. I am not a full-time Talmudist, and there are
dimensions of Talmud study which lie beyond my competence. Nevertheless, this limited experience left me convinced that some of the obstacles to effective Talmud instruction usually cited are not real, or, if actual,
can be overcome. Worthwhile academic results were achieved for the
effort invested. This experience prompted me to look into the reasons
for the relative neglect of Talmud's study in our Judaica programs at a
time when other areas of Jewish studies are receiving considerable attention. Several factors must be considered:

1) It is hard to secure teachers of Talmud who are suitable for
teaching in the university. By this we mean scholars whose training has
prepared them to approach the study of Talmud critically; whose understanding of it has been secularized, so that they may transmit it as a
humanistic discipline. What is here required is the integration of the
traditional fluency in Talmudic text, which brings with it an intimate
familiarity with its terminology and dialectic, with the ability to bring to
bear on that text the tools of modern scholarship.

2) The relevance of Talmudic literature has not been appreciated
adequately by many of those responsible for Judaic programs in American universities. I have been repeatedly taken aback to discover that
even masters in other areas of Judaic studies retain antiquated notions of
what Talmud study is, and seem to be dominated by images and associations that turn them off whenever one speaks of teaching Talmudic
texts in the university.

Many of today's Judaic scholars studied Talmud under conditions
which they would hardly think of reproducing in the American university.
The relatively few masters in the field of Talmud have failed, in my
opinion, to interpret the relevance of their findings to the corps of Judaica
men in the universities, nor have they sought to present their enlightened
understanding of the subject to the general scholarly community in broad
humanistic terms.

3) The secularization process in the study of Talmud has lagged
behind other areas of Judaic studies. This is more the case in America
than it is in Israel, where the animus of a Hebraic culture lends broader
relevance to all that is Judaic. When one introduces a Bible course into a
university curriculum he is treating an area of inquiry shared by Jews and
non-Jews alike, and one which has a history as a secular discipline.
Liberal Protestant scholarship secularized the study of Bible long ago, and

Jewish scholars building on the achievements of their non-Jewish counterparts, have added new dimensions to Bible research and have done something that Christian scholarship might not have been able to do even if it had wanted to: It demonstrated that the Bible is a cornerstone of Jewish civilization and peoplehood. The same kind of progress cannot be attested to for the study of Talmud. This is not because the tools for critical study are lacking, relatively speaking, or because Talmud has not attracted great minds. It is because Talmud has almost always been studied under particularly Jewish auspices. At a time when other areas of Judaic studies, only recently viewed by the academy as the parochial concern of Jews, have become accepted into the humanities curriculum, the study of Talmud continues to remain a thing apart.

4) The study of Talmud is the victim of the polarization of intellectual life which characterizes contemporary American Jewry. The large majority of those who study Talmud in America today do so in yeshivot. With very few exceptions the American yeshivah is out of touch with recent Jewish scholarship. Some yeshivot even oppose secular studies on the college level. There are a few institutions wherein one notes an incipient secularization of Talmudic and other Judaic studies. Yeshiva University comes to mind. It was initially committed to secular studies, but until very recently, this commitment was not applied to the substance of the Judaic literary tradition. Now some graduate programs have been established which, if properly conducted, will produce Talmud scholars for the university. Links with academically enlightened leaders in the Yeshivah community must be sought earnestly by those directing university programs in Judaica.

To understand the present situation some background is necessary. The Lithuanian yeshivah actually began the secularization process even before the emergence of the *Wissenschaft* movement. In the school of the Gaon of Vilna, methods of Talmud research were perfected which represented the crystallization of centuries of critical study. Only two elements were lacking: 1) An historical perspective, not as regards the history of the Talmudic texts, but as pertains to an awareness of those real Jewish societies whose ethos found expression in Talmudic literature; 2) The comparative method in philology, literary analysis, and in the study of institutions which, when applied properly, adds to our understanding of the text and sharpens the historical perspective as well.

These desiderata were missing in the yeshivah, even at its best. Consequently, the yeshivah experienced a brain drain. We do not speak here of all those who abandoned the study of Torah altogether, but only of the minority who stuck to the study of Talmud, but who came to realize that it would be given new life and meaning only if secular wisdom were applied to it. Such students left the yeshivah to study in Western universities. Some of them are the great masters of our generation and of the last few generations, who have transformed our understanding of the Talmudic text. The intellectual heirs of the Gaon are not to be found in the contemporary yeshivah!

The yeshivah has been unable to preceive the ultimate logic of the Gaon's methodology. It had failed to realize that a fruitful methodology must grow and change, or else shrivel up. The yeshivah now exists in a prolonged *décadence*. The "single ray of light" of which Bialik spoke in his poem never penetrated to it! There is, however, another viewpoint. Without wishing to romanticize the yeshivah or to overlook its serious intellectual limitations and the unfortunate rigidity of its socio-religious environment, I have never ceased to believe that it embodied certain academic values worth reflecting upon with reference to the university.

To study Talmud with the objective of ascertaining what Jewish law demands of one, or of the community, in terms of Halakhah, is to pursue an essentially religious discipline. To study Talmud with the objective of comprehending the underlying principles of Halakhah, of penetrating the systematic thought world of the Sages without direct regard for its practical applicability, is to pursue an essentially secular discipline. The Lithuanian yeshivah committed itself to the latter approach long ago! Two orders of the Talmud were classically emphasized in the best of the Lithuanian yeshivot, *Nashim* and *Nezikin*. This was because these orders contained those *sûgeyôt,* or architectonic units of dialectical discussion, which hold the key to the Talmudic legal system. Otherwise, it is Mo'ed which informs us of the Sabbath and Festivals, and other orders which deal with Kashrut and family purity, and these would be the most immediately relevant to Jewish living. Though Talmud study was conceived as a religious duty in terms of the motivations and spiritual goals of the yeshivah student and his teachers, the actual intellectual pursuit was executed for its own sake, as a systematic discipline.

Can the students and faculties of the contemporary yeshivot play a role in the university? Despite many indications to the contrary, I, for one, would not be ready to abandon the effort. We dare not ignore the yeshivah, and we might be pleasantly surprised to find, in certain quarters, a readiness to broaden scholarly horizons. In the larger scholarly context, the time is also ripe for unwrapping the Talmud. Christendom has finally become concerned with what happened within Judaism after the Advent. The relevance of Rabbinic literature is now accepted without contradiction. We now have a singular opportunity to share the wealth of Talmudic literature with the scholarly academy, and with the larger society as well. We already have some models upon which to base further efforts. A few well-qualified Talmud scholars, who never attended a yeshivah, are entering the university as instructors. In America, it is the special program of the Jewish Theological Seminary of America, with its research-connected facilities, that has done the most to produce young Talmud scholars who have been afforded the opportunity for intensive Talmud study along critical lines. Some have been encouraged to seek comparative competence in related languages and literatures, in history, and law.

Such programs must be established as part of the Judaic curricula in universities. In so doing, one educational consideration requires paramount attention. It is educationally unsound to establish a sequence through which one first studies the Talmud in the "old way" until he achieves fluency, and only then is introduced to the new methodology. This is what occurred in the personal chronology of almost all of the modern Talmud scholars until very recently. For them it was unavoidable. We don't know of all those who never made the transition! This sequence surely has no place in our academic efforts. From the very outset, the student should be shown the potentialities of his pursuit so that as his mastery of the text increases, his method becomes more and more refined. The aperceptive mass should not be overemphasized to the detriment of developing proper thought processes. The sea of the Talmud is admittedly vast, but no more so than Assyriology, Islamic studies, or classics, to name a few ponderous humanistic disciplines. Scholars are being trained in those fields, and they can be trained, as well, in Talmud if there is the commitment to doing so. The status of Talmud study in the present Judaic curriculum of the American university is, unfortunately, not commensurate with the historical importance of Talmudic literature in Jewish civilization. The flight from Talmud must be arrested by improved methods of study and by a legitimate interpretation of relevance on all levels. The polarization of traditionalism and modernism within Jewish life must not be perpetuated by default of efforts to bridge it. This is all the more reason for moving ahead now in the formation of an association of professors of Judaica, so that this and similar problems can be attacked in a coordinated manner.

THE PROBLEM OF CONTEMPORARY
JEWISH STUDIES

MARSHALL SKLARE
Yeshiva University
Professor of Sociology

WHY are contemporary Jewish studies different from all other Jewish studies? All other Jewish studies are taught on the university level, but it is difficult to find either general universities or institutions of higher Jewish learning which offer courses in contemporary Jewish studies. All other Jewish studies are cultivated by full-time experts, but this is not generally the case with contemporary Jewish studies. With all other Jewish studies it is simple to advise the novice on how to become an expert, but since contemporary Jewish studies is a subject not generally taught or cultivated by full-time experts, it is difficult to say precisely how one gains professional competence.

Is the invitation to discuss contemporary Jewish studies at this colloquium, then, out of order? Perhaps so. If the invitation was a mistake we believe that it was proffered with good intentions; , with a secret conviction that a Judaic curriculum which exludes contemporary studies is an incomplete curriculum.

Certainly the field of contemporary Jewish studies is alive, even if it is not entirely well. There is an extensive literature on the subject. There is a journal entitled *The Jewish Journal of Sociology* and another one named *Jewish Social Studies*. Data relevant to contemporary Jewish studies is accumulating rapidly; the retrieval problem is already a formidable one. Institutes in contemporary Jewish studies exist at the Hebrew University, at Brandeis, and at several European universities.

In summary, contemporary Jewish studies—by which we mean the study of present-day Jewry and its immediate antecedents—is a reality. In some respects it may even be considered a growing discipline. However, its historical development and its present position are in sharp contrast to most other areas of Jewish studies.

I.

What is the essential difference between contemporary Jewish studies and the field of Jewish studies as a whole? The difference hinges on the fact that Jewish studies are, by and large, past-oriented. The field of Jewish studies has its origin in the classical tradition of Jewish learning with its concern for *halakhah*. Thus it comes by its orientation towards the past naturally. Such orientation was in no way modified by the innovations introduced by *Wissenschaft des Judentums*. While the method of Jewish learning in our own day may be as different as that of the *yeshivah* and the graduate school of the secular university, the curricula of both institutions are centered on the study of the Jewish past. Furthermore, the values of the Jewish scholar may vary from that of the religionist who sees himself as a servant of God to the secularist who sees himself as the servant of his discipline, but both are as one in centering their research on the study of the Jewish past.

Wissenschaft des Judentums greatly expanded the subject matter of Jewish learning and decisively changed its methodology. Yet it appears as highly oriented to the past as was traditional rabbinic learning. It is true that the founding fathers of modern Jewish studies saw *Wissenschaft des Judentums* as offering something of great value to their contemporaries. They were also much concerned with issues such as Jewish rights and Jewish-Gentile relations. But the point is that they did not see the Jews of their own time as subjects for research. To be sure, modern Jewish scholarship developed at a time when the social sciences were in their infancy, and when it was possible for scholars to be insulated from their influence. Yet the nub of the matter is that the founders of modern Jewish studies were thoroughgoing classicists. Or, to put it in another way, they were contemporary versions of the traditional rabbinic scholar.

We may assume that today most practitioners of modern Jewish studies are aware of its existence in a field of scholarship. Some might even agree that work in this field should be encouraged. Yet many of the most eminent practitioners of modern Jewish scholarship seem as distant from contemporary studies as were the founders of *Wissenschaft des Judentums* over a century ago. One senses in them a feeling of discomfort about and a kind of resistance to contemporary Jewish studies. This does not seem to be entirely a generalized rejection of the new. Other post-*Wissenschaft* specialties have been accepted by the practitioners of modern Jewish studies. Thus the specialty we call modern Hebrew literature seems to have developed without incident. Slowly but surely it has been introduced into the curriculum of institutions which aim at offering a well-rounded program of Judaic studies.

It would seem that the discomfort and resistance of the scholarly establishment is more than simply the status deprivation experienced by practitioners of the humanities when confronted by proponents of newer and ever-expanding disciplines. The specialist in contemporary Jewish studies may unwittingly serve as an irritant, upsetting the symmetry of the past-orientation of modern Jewish studies. It may be that, despite his modernity, the Jewish scholar may wish to put out of mind the question of the balance between the study of the past and of the present. He may feel that there is nothing about the present which is worthy of study —that the contemporary age is debased, brutish. Only when the Jewish scholar is confronted with the necessity of taking some responsibility, himself, for an aspect of contemporary Jewish studies, is he forced to consider how past-oriented Jewish scholarship is. Characteristically though, he does not seek to redress the balance. Louis Finkelstein's testimony is a case in point:

> Some years ago, I undertook to prepare a comprehensive work describing the whole phenomenon of Judaism. It was to include a history of the Jews, a description of their present condition, a discussion of their contribution to civilization and role in it, and an outline of their beliefs and practices. . . . What surprised me . . . was the dearth of information about Jews today. There are probably a hundred people, and more, whose profession it is to discover all that can be known about the Jews in Jerusalem in the first century; there does not seem to be one who has the same duty for the Jews of New York in the twentieth century.[1]

Not only does tension occur because Jewish scholarship has been so past-oriented, but there is also the difficulty that contemporary Jewish studies have their origin in the social sciences. While *Wissenschaft des Judentums* prided itself on the fact that it was open-minded—in apposition of course to traditional rabbinic scholarship—it did not take kindly to the social sciences. To earlier generations of modern Jewish scholars these sciences seemed debased; they appeared to involve a denigration of noble aspects of Jewish culture. As some viewed it, the social sciences were guilty of introducing what were, at best, irrelevancies and, at the worst, perversions.

An incident related by President Shazar in his autobiography highlights the problem. In 1909 Zalman Shazar was a student at the Academy of Jewish Studies in St. Petersburg (because of government policy the school was officially titled "Institute of Oriental Studies"). Confronted by the negative attitude which the administration of the Academy held towards the social sciences, Shazar proceeded to lead a student revolt. He describes the affair as follows:

> One of the disciplines which we students felt to be lacking and necessary was historical study of the social and economic life of Jews in the lands of the Diaspora. It was not easy to find a specialist in this field, and when Dubnow, whom we had impressed with our desire for such study, came at last to tell us that there was a fine young scholar available, Dr. M. L. Wischnitzer of Vienna, he added with restrained sadness that he feared the Baron [Baron David Günzburg, the moving spirit of the Academy] would not agree to open the doors of the Academy to a course stressing the "new-fangled" social and economic approach.
>
> We decided to try to appeal to Baron Günzburg directly. . . . He agreed to receive a delegation. There were three of us, and to this day I remember with absolute clarity the talk between us and the fatherly Baron. I had been charged with opening our case. There in the Baron's study, facing the picture of Maimonides, I spoke of the need for this new discipline and of the young scholar who was available. Excitedly, the Baron rose from his chair, leaned against the doorpost opening onto his great library . . . and said . . . : "Dear ones, I am deeply grieved by this request of yours. I am certain that you have no intention . . . of causing me unhappiness, and it is very difficult for me to say no to you. But how can I hide my concern from you? You have come here to study the nature and destiny of the Jewish people—and now I hear you asking to be taught what occupations Jews were compelled to engage in. . . . It is as if a scholar had been asked to lecture to you on Kant, and then, instead of teaching you the *Critique of Pure Reason*, spent his time describing the restaurant Kant frequented and the kind of cutlets his wife gave him. And it is not Kant you are studying, but that sublime people God chose for His own! Do you really think it is so important to know exactly when the gentiles permitted us to engage in trade and when those malicious people forced us to be money-lenders? What good will the information do you? And wouldn't it be a pity to spend your precious time on this when there are still so many rooms in the mansion of Jewish scholarship that are closed to you and so many great books waiting for you?" As he spoke, he pointed to the tens of rooms filled with bookshelves from floor to ceiling, [an] endless, infinite treasure of books. . . .
>
> . . . Walking excitedly across the room between the desk and the books [he] suddenly stood still and went on even more bitingly: "If you do research on horses—there is such a science, too—it is obviously

very important to investigate what fodder should be put in the horses' crib: oats or barley. But when the subject of your study is the wisdom of the chosen people, do you think that their fodder . . . should concern you?"[2]

II.

The singularity of contemporary Jewish studies becomes evident once we realize that its development is not closely related to the evolution of Jewish scholarship. None of the founders of modern Jewish scholarship in Germany made a contribution to the field, and none of the pioneers in the United States interested themselves in the area. If the impetus for the creation of contemporary Jewish studies did not come from *Wissenchaft des Judentums,* then where did it arise?

The natural place to look is to the social sciences themselves, as well as, to some extent, to the field of contemporary history. Since Jews were active in the development of the social sciences it is conceivable that some Jewish social scientists would turn to Jewish topics. This has, indeed, been the case, although we shall later inquire into the reasons why more were not interested in Jewish topics. Yet the fact of the matter is that, if contemporary Jewish studies were merely a kind of Jewish fallout from the social sciences, they would constitute more of an intellectual curiosity than a topic for serious discussion.

The student revolt led by Shazar at the Academy of Jewish Studies in St. Petersburg—a revolt aided and abetted by a radical faculty member, Simon Dubnow—clues us in to the direction in which to look for the impetus to contemporary Jewish studies. The incident is a significant illustration of how Jewish nationalism made devoted students of *Wissenschaft des Judentums* dissatisfied with a curriculum which had just been introduced in Eastern Europe, and was merely a half-century old even in Western Europe. The new curriculum at first dazzled those who—like Shazar—had been reared in the tradition of classical Jewish learning. However, Jewish nationalism in general, and Zionism in particular, soon made that curriculum seem less than perfect to its students. *But the contribution to Jewish studies of nationalism and Zionism was even greater, for it supplied the most substantial single impetus to the field of contemporary Jewish studies.*[3]

Nationalism impelled individuals to evaluate the Jewish condition. In the course of attempting such an evaluation it became evident that data was needed. In order to gather meaningful data, conceptualization was necessary. Furthermore, Jewish nationalism looked upon the Jews as a problem; nationalism viewed the Jews as being a problem due to the position which they occupied in society rather than because of the idiosyncrasies of individual Jews. Furthermore, nationalism maintained that the solution to the Jewish problem lay in the direction of group survival rather than group disappearance (some stressed that, even if disappearance were desirable, it was impossible). In sum, Jewish nationalism prepared the groundwork for contemporary Jewish studies—without the orientations which it provided, systematic work in the field could not have emerged.

The contributions of Arthur Ruppin (1876–1943) make manifest the influence of the Zionist perspective. Ruppin, who may be regarded as the pioneer of contemporary Jewish studies, was an official of various Zionist institutions during much of the time that he was active on the scholarly scene. His sociological work was informed with a Zionist perspective even as his efforts to establish settlements in Palestine were characterized by a sociological perspective.

In his books Ruppin constantly compared Jews of one country with those of another. He conceived of the Jews as a worldwide people, though of course like so many others of the period he focused upon the Jews of Western and Eastern Europe, and upon Jews who had emigrated from Europe. His data was derived not only from his library research but also from his contacts and travels as a Zionist official. And when he traveled, he observed. Thus: "The Jewish appearance especially of the small and middle-sized Polish town is enhanced by the Jews having their shops and offices in the chief thoroughfares, and doing a good deal of their business in the street."[4] As the pioneer of contemporay Jewish studies, Ruppin established a journal. He also encouraged others to interest themselves in the field. The pity of it is that some of those who are in his debt today hardly know his name.

In 1926 Ruppin began lecturing on Jewish sociology at the Hebrew University. The previous year a graduate student at the University of Chicago, Louis Wirth (1897–1952), completed a doctoral dissertation in the field of what we now call contemporary Jewish studies. Wirth's dissertation was published in 1928 under the title *The Ghetto*. It became one of the most popular items in the series of sociological monographs published by the University of Chicago Press. At about the same time Ruppin began to prepare his Hebrew University lectures for publication. They were published in 1930–31, in Berlin, in two volumes under the title *Die Soziologie der Juden*. A Hebrew edition appeared almost immediately, as did a condensed version in English. In any case Ruppin was already well-known, for he had published his first book on contemporary Jewish studies in German in 1904, and English, Hebrew, and Italian translations had followed.

The contrast between Arthur Ruppin and Louis Wirth is instructive. One was the Zionist founder of Jewish sociology. The other, a non-Zionist if not an anti-Zionist, became the most influential Jew of his time in American sociology and a President of the American Sociological Association.

Ruppin's work is characterized by the fact that he employed the same basic approach throughout his career. Despite this limitation, and the fact that he was heavily involved in public service and private business, his interest and productivity in the field of contemporary Jewish studies extended over more than three decades. The Jewish people, which he saw as a living organism constantly growing and ever changing, was always an object of fascination to him.

Wirth, on the other hand, never did any substantial work in the field of contemporary Jewish studies after he had completed his dissertation. Although his early life was spent in the Orthodox environment of a Rhineland village, his convictions shifted radically after his arrival in the United States at the age of fourteen. In the closing pages of *The Ghetto* he makes clear his view that the Jewish community no longer constituted a natural community but rather an anachronism prolonged by Gentile prejudice.[5] According to his daughter, Wirth was ". . . the first member of his family to marry a non-Jew. . . . Wirth's assimilationist inclinations and principles, like those of his wife, partly derived from their common reaction against dogmatism and provincial ethnocentrism. Their two daughters were to be encouraged in agnosticism with audible atheistic overtones, at the same time that they were to acquire a 'generalized minority' ethnic identification."[6] Lacking a nationalist perspective Wirth increasingly came to look upon the Jews as a dead rather than a living phenomenon and he turned his attention to what he felt were more significant topics: the need for social planning, better cities, and improved understanding between racial groups.[7]

Despite admiration for Israel, most of today's Jewish sociologists do not share Arthur Ruppin's concerns; but neither do they have a great deal in common with Louis Wirth. They do not come from pious homes. They have not recently emerged from the darkness of the village into the light of the modern world. Coming from the city they do not need to celebrate urbanism as a way of life. And unlike Wirth, who sought to work within the power structure and who never engaged in radical social criticism in spite of a brief encounter with Marxism, a noticeable segment of today's Jewish sociologists pride themselves on their aliena- tion. Finally, unlike Wirth, many are vocal about their Jewish identity —even ethnocentric in a certain way. They use what Yiddish they know with abandon and they proudly instruct their Gentile colleagues in its mysteries. The net effect of all of this is that, instead of denigrating the ghetto as Wirth had done, today's Jewish sociologists tend to admire it. The ghetto was community; it was authentic. In the ghetto the Jews did their own thing; life was with people.

A little more than three decades after *The Ghetto* was published a volume which constitutes a kind of sequel to Wirth's book made its appearance. I refer to *Children of the Gilded Ghetto* by Kramer and Leventman.[8] Nostalgia for the immigrant era when Jews lived on the margins of society and were presumed to be rooted in Jewish culture is implicit in *Children of the Gilded Ghetto*. Although the residents of the ghetto were poor and struggling they led a rich and rewarding existence. The second generation, however, became prosperous. American-born Jews led sterile lives; prosperity has made them vulgar, conservative, and self-satisfied. They live in gilded ghettos and they are part of the estab- lishment, or think that they are.[9] Oh, for the good old days on Manhat- tan's Lower East Side or Wirth's Maxwell Street district on Chicago's Old West Side! In sum, the perspective of many of today's Jewish soci- ologists appears to be as biased in its own way as was the perspective of an earlier generation.

III

The issue at present confronting contemporary Jewish studies is the problem of how such studies are to be stimulated—how they are to be encouraged to reach a level which will make them comparable to other fields of modern Jewish scholarship.

One approach is that of having their development take place within the social sciences. If such a development is to occur, the attitude of the Jewish professoriat is crucial. Since Jews in the United States do not pose a social problem in the conventional sense—contemporary Jewish studies are the business of the Jewish professor—it is the exceptional Gentile professor who has any concern with this area of scholarship. One such professor was Robert E. Park. As Louis Wirth's mentor he seems to have been influential in steering Wirth to a Jewish topic. Park was a great Jewish studies enthusiast. He viewed the Jews as constituting the ideal type of minority group, and he felt that a study of their history and situation and of their response to them, would be salutary for all students, Gentile as well as Jewish. Very few Jewish social scientists have shared his unique enthusiasm. In fact, despite the present mood in respect to Jewishness there has been a persistent tendency for Jewish social scientists to perceive Jewish studies as being in conflict with their professional identity. As Lipset has pointed out:

> The failure of Jewish social scientists to engage in research on the Jews reflects their desire to be perceived as American rather than Jewish intellectuals. To write in depth about the Jewish community would seemingly expose them to being identified as . . . individuals who are too preoccupied with an ethnic identity, and who lack the universalistic orientation prized by social scientists and American intellectuals generally.[10]

While this statement is certainly correct, we must realize at the same time that there have been a significant number of individuals who have written in depth about the Jewish community.[11] It is this group which is of special interest to us. We notice, here, a curious phenomenon: while such professors write about Jews they do not teach about them. Thus, sociologists capable of giving instruction in contemporary Jewish studies have hesitated to introduce courses on the subject. This despite the fact that the sociological curriculum has proliferated during the past two decades and new fields and areas of study are constantly being introduced. Even those who hold professorial posts at universities where there are many thousands of Jewish students, and where a variety of courses in Jewish studies are offered, have hesitated to take the initiative in this matter. Such professors have chosen rather to pursue contemporary Jewish studies more as a personal interest than as a professional or public responsibility. It appears that confining one's teaching to the same set of courses offered by one's colleagues allows such a sociologist to present a universalistic face to the "academic-world-at-large." Of course his intimates understand that his interest in writing about Jewish problems is closely connected with his feelings about Jewish identity.

The situation in Israel suggests that the reticence of such sociologists is not simply a response to being a Jew in a Gentile world. While Ruppin's work is being continued at the Hebrew University, it is centered in a specialized facility—the Institute of Contemporary Jewry—where it cannot be confused with the work of the institution's regular social-science departments. Apparently the offering of a program of courses on contemporary Jewish studies would conflict with the self-image of Israeli academicians as universalistic social scientists.

The comparative absence of courses in contemporary Jewish studies in the United States must be regarded as a serious problem, for a discipline which exists outside of the university curriculum cannot long endure. Thus it is the responsibility of those social scientists who consider themselves to be seriously interested in Jewish studies to discard their universalistic face and to introduce Jewish studies into the course offerings of their departments.

We must recognize, however, that the prognosis for the development of contemporary Jewish studies under the sheltering arms of social-science departments is only fair. As the Hatchett affair at New York University and other such incidents demonstrate, one should not overestimate the sense of Jewish dignity and self-assertion of Jewish professors and administrators, including many who consider themselves "positive" Jews and are widely regarded as such.

The movement for Black studies may of course embolden Jewish faculty members to make a demand for Jewish studies. But it may also have the effect of making them more wary than they already are of presenting anything but a universalistic face, of making them even more hesitant to introduce new areas of possible contention; and it may serve to further justify their feeling that the time is not right for the presentation of specifically Jewish demands.

If contemporary Jewish studies are not developed within the context of social-science departments, another possibility exists. They might develop in departments of Jewish studies or wherever Jewish studies are located as, for example, in departments of religion. While the development of contemporary Jewish studies in social-science departments is hampered by the professional self-image of the Jewish social scientist, another kind of problem is encountered in the "Jewish" department; in order to encourage the continued development of contemporary Jewish studies the scholar of modern Jewish studies must break with traditional definitions of what Judaic studies are. Of course, the more of a Jewish nationalist the Jewish scholar is and the more of the survivalist he is, the more concerned he will be about the study of contemporary Jewish life. Hence, the more eager he will be to recruit the necessary specialists into his ranks, and the more agreeable he will be to granting them legitimacy. Other factors which facilitate this process are security in one's scholarly identity and a personality relatively flexible and free of rigidity.

Locating contemporary Jewish studies in departments of Jewish studies or in departments where Jewish studies are concentrated might be highly beneficial to the social scientist. Generally the social-science preparation of such academicians is much superior to their Jewish preparation. Many have not been exposed to systematic Jewish study on a secondary-school or college level. Jewishly speaking their work is sometimes naive; at other times it betrays embarrassing mistakes. In some instances the right questions are not asked: the questions which are posed are those which occur to someone from the social sciences who has a feeling for Jewish identity, but who lacks disciplined study in Jewish history, religion, and culture.

While some of these deficiencies may be remedied by association with a Jewish-studies department, there is no denying that the social scientist who leaves his natural habitat exposes himself to grave dangers. For example, his situation is much more difficult than that of the social scientist who leaves his department to accept an appointment with a hospital or a medical school. In such cases the social scientist is generally a member of a team of social scientists; he is also part of a recognized specialty in his discipline, such as "medical sociology." The social scientist who moves into a Jewish-studies department, however, soon confronts an intellectual problem: he is away from where the action in his discipline is taking place. He labors under the fear, and the real possibility, that, sooner or later, his contacts will wither away. Furthermore, he fears that by virtue of his isolation the quality of his work will suffer. He also labors under an identity problem: he can no longer present a universalistic face to the "academic-world-at-large." He no longer feels as comfortable as before in his old professional haunts, but at the same time he is not really part of the Jewish scholarly establishment. He may find that, instead of studying the Jewish group as an example of marginality, he himself has come to exemplify this role!

Whether the practitioners of Judaic studies will seek to foster the development of contemporary Jewish studies and will attempt to induce social scientists to join their departments remains to be seen. Perhaps it is unwise to place too great a trust in the wisdom, magnanimity, and sense of Jewishness of the practitioners of modern Jewish scholarship. Furthermore, it is by no means clear that the social scientist will accept the invitation of Judaic scholars, if and when it is proffered. What then of the Jewish student? It is conceivable that the hesitancies of Jewish administrators and of Jewish faculty—those who teach the social sciences as well as those who teach Jewish studies—may be overcome by pressures originating from a "third force": the student body.

Some sixty years ago Zalman Shazar and his fellow students succeeded in their objective of modifying the curriculum of the St. Petersburg Academy of Jewish Studies. Soon after the confrontation with the Baron, Professor Wischnitzer was invited to offer a course entitled "The Economic History of the Jews." Baron David Günzberg, as it happened, was a true aristocrat. While his hold over the students of the Academy was absolute—not only was he the sole financial support of the institution but he had gone so far as to arrange residence permits to enable students who lacked them to live in St. Petersburg (by instructing his steward to bribe police inspectors where necessary)—the Baron nevertheless felt that he had no right to deprive the students of knowledge which they sought to acquire. Consequently, and in spite of his aversion to the social sciences, he proceeded to invite Wischnitzer to join the faculty. And he also invited visitors about whom he had strong reservations, but whom the students adored. These visitors, incidentally, included such notorious radicals as Chaim Nachman Bialik!

The students of the Academy believed that the approach to Jewish history of the scholars whose books they had studied did not speak to their situation. They had need for someone who saw Jewish history differently from a Jost or a Graetz. They required a type of approach to Jewish history that even so advanced a thinker as Dubnow could not fully supply. We must remember that before he came to St. Petersburg Shazar had carried out missions for the Poale Zion, and he had translated some of Borochov from Russian into Yiddish. Other students had been similarly involved in the Jewish social movements of the time. Thus, they all felt it was crucial that they know precisely how it was that Jews had become involved in trade and in moneylending. Given this need they could not be satisfied with the Baron's conception of *Wissenschaft des Judentums*.

If Shazar and his contemporaries were critical of the *Wissenschaft* of their day we must expect that our students should be equally critical of the *Wissenschaft* which we have to offer them. If criticism is absent it reflects negatively both upon us and upon them. Above all, we must remember that if Jewish studies in the American university are to have a vital future it will be because they fulfill a need which the young Jew feels. Thus the push to the study of Judaica must originate in the desire to explore personal identity. It follows then that the future of Jewish studies in the American university will be abortive if they move too far in the direction of becoming a pure and impersonal science.

Given this impetus for the study of Judaica, the need for contemporary

Jewish studies will become evident: in order to plumb his identity the young Jew will not only have to be familiar with the Jewish classics and the history of his remote ancestors, but he will have to study himself and his immediate forebears.

This would not be the first time that the need for identity has stimulated new developments in scholarship. Was not the establishment of *Wissenschaft des Judentums* connected with the identity needs of Jewish intellectuals in Germany in the nineteenth century? And in the present century, has not the efflorescence of the study of the Biblical period in Israel been a result of the Israeli search for identity?

There may be some who fear that concern and involvement with the identity problem, and by extension with the welfare of the Jewish community, will pervert the nature of modern Jewish scholarship. Let them be strong and of good courage, for the opposite is the case. Without such concern modern Jewish scholarship will be neither modern nor Jewish.

NOTES

1. *Proceedings of the Rabbinical Assembly of America,* Vol. XIII (1949) p. 121.

2. Zalman Shazar, *Morning Stars,* Jewish Publication Society of America (Philadelphia: 1967), pp. 188–190.

3. Diaspora nationalism has also given impetus to contemporary Jewish studies, as the work of the Yiddish Scientific Institute—YIVO demonstrates.

4. Arthur Ruppin, *The Jews in the Modern World,* Macmillan & Co. (London: 1934), p. 38.

5. See Louis Wirth, *The Ghetto,* University of Chicago Press (Chicago: 1892), esp. pp. 263–81.

6. Elizabeth Wirth Marvick, "Louis Wirth: A Biographical Memorandum," Albert J. Reiss, Jr., ed., in *Louis Wirth: On Cities and Social Life,* University of Chicago Press (Chicago: 1964), p. 337.

7. In 1943—perhaps in response to Nazism—Wirth published what was for him a kind of homage to Jewish tenacity in the face of persecution: "Education for Survival: The Jews," *American Journal of Sociology,* Vol. XLVIII, No. 6 (May 1943), pp. 682–91.

8. Judith R. Kramer and Seymour Leventman, *Children of the Gilded Ghetto,* Yale University Press (New Haven: 1961).

9. One of the strongest expressions of such sentiments can be found in an article by a leading Jewish sociologist: Melvin M. Tumin "Conservative Trends in American Jewish Life," *Judaism,* Vol. XIII, No. 2 (Spring 1964), pp. 131–42.

10. Seymour Martin Lipset, "The Study of Jewish Communities in a Comparative Context," *The Jewish Journal of Sociology,* Vol. V, No. 2, (December 1963), p. 163.

11. Of course one topic is written about endlessly—the *kibbutz.* But if there are already more books, articles, and dissertations on the *kibbutz* than there are *kibbutzim,* the topic is surely the exception. Most investigators have little interest in the *kibbutz* as an institution in a Jewish society. Rather, their interest is in the *kibbutz* as an experiment in collective living.

MODERN HEBREW LITERATURE

ARNOLD J. BAND
*University of California
in Los Angeles
Professor of Hebrew Literature*

I

As the representative of modern Hebrew literature at this colloquium, I must confess to an inescapable feeling of uneasiness as I stand before you, for I know that my discipline, though popular with students, is probably the least understood and respected of all the disciplines in this area. This feeling, I can assure you, is shared by many of my colleagues and is not simply a manifestation of my paranoia. Serious scholarship has a venerable tradition in the Jewish world and modern scientific scholarship—as we have heard so many times in the past few days—has enjoyed 150 years of experience with Judaic texts. In my field, however, serious scholarship and criticism is relatively new and deals with material written only a few decades ago or only yesterday. Since academic scholarship is usually conservative, particularly in the Humanities, what is new or deals with new material is often viewed with suspicion or scorn.

It is very lonely, let me assure you, on the fringes of any society, even the academic society, yet there is a virtue in this loneliness; from this position one gains perspective, one is free to look at the academic world almost as an outsider, to see it as it is, to accept its methods, but reject its inhibitions. If we are sensitive, the material we study shapes our response to it. We are attracted to those verbal dramatizations of the infinite variety of human behavior. We are, therefore, forced into the very heartland of human experience, the proper domain of humanistic studies. From this central peak, the preoccupations of more traditional scholars often seem trivial, even dehumanizing. I raise the question of humanity and humaneness at the very beginning of this paper precisely because so many of us have assumed, either in prepared papers or in casual remarks over the past few days, that American humanistic scholarship (or any humanistic scholarship, for that matter) was the summum bonum, or something close to it. We have not yet asked if this is true. Our students obviously do not think it is. And to bring the matter a bit closer to home, let me quote this passage from George Steiner's *To Civilize our Gentlemen:*

> Recently one of my colleagues, an eminent scholar, inquired of me, with genuine bafflement, why someone trying to establish himself in an English-literature faculty should refer so often to concentration camps; why they were in any way relevant. They are profoundly relevant, and before we can go on teaching we must surely ask ourselves: are the humanities humane and, if so, why did they fail before the night? . . . Kierkegaard made a cruel distinction, but we could do worse than bear it in mind when we enter a room to give a lecture on Shakespeare or Coleridge, or Yeats: "There are two ways, one is to suffer; the other is to become a professor of the fact that another suffers."

If these remarks have any validity for a professor of English literature—and I think that they do—they obviously should mean something to a colloquium of professors of Judaica only twenty-five years after Auschwitz. Vietnam and Biafra are not on our agenda, and I am not suggesting that they should be, but they compel us to question some of the assumptions of our lives. Literary criticism, I have discovered, does force me to question, time and again; the very existence of modern Hebrew literature raises many problems which transcend the purely "objective" study of texts. The following remarks should be understood in this context.

Any serious scholar or teacher of modern Hebrew literature in an American university is constantly impressed by several facts which are generated by the peculiar nature of his discipline, and determine his attitude towards it.

(A) He must be more attuned to Israel, its writers and scholars (i.e., to the *living literary tradition* there) than any other type of Judaics scholar in America: his intellectual community is there, not here. America, unfortunately, barely exists today as a center of Hebrew creativity and there are few men here *seriously* engaged in the study of modern Hebrew literature. I must, therefore, direct my attention to certain developments in Israel and, only then, can I turn to specific problems of the instructor of modern Hebrew literature in American universities.

(B) His colleagues in other fields of literary study haven't the slightest idea of the material and problems which concern him. While he might—indeed, should—be able to share their interests, they cannot share his, for they cannot read Hebrew. Ironically, modern Hebrew literature, so prominent in the attempt to escape the intellectual ghetto, ends up ghettoized in the secular university.

(C) He works in a field in which there have been no great masters, no Baron, no Wolfson, no Scholem, no Baer; in brief, no tradition of scholarship upon which he can rely and build. He always works from the very beginning and pays a price for this lack of tradition.

(D) As stated above, his field of study is, at once, one of the most popular (among Jews) yet least respected areas of Judaica. Indeed, the opposing poles of popular pleasure and scholarly respect, of public notoriety and cautious acclaim, of moral engagement and academic objectivity are the extremes between which he must tread an uneasy, broken path.

II

The last of these four existential facts is the most intriguing and merits further discussion. The popularity among students or the Hebrew-reading public is engendered partly by the pleasures of reading contemporary or recent literature, and partly by the fascination with what's contemporary or (in the case of some American Jewish students) with what's Israeli. Among many academicians, however, popularity breeds contempt or, at least, suspicion. We in the academic world are relatively few, often beleaguered, usually elitist; we glory in the esoteric, cultivate our own philological gardens, deplore most of mass culture. In general, we love the antique for its own sake, valuing an ancient grocery bill more than a significant modern novel.

Inertial academic opposition to other modern literatures has been overcome by the establishment of programs, journals, and all the known paraphernalia of scholarship during the past two generations, particularly since World War II. Regrettably, the same is not true for modern Hebrew literature, not in Israel and certainly not here. While impressive strides have been made during the past few years in Israel towards the establishment of reasonable scholarly criteria in this area, the achievement is still too new, too tenuous, to be recognized as a permanent trend. The lack of a solid scholarly tradition is a liability, but it is also an asset for, freed of the encrustations of time, each man can exercise his own critical judgment with less inhibition, and his unique, perhaps oblique perspective allows him to see, often with astonishing clarity, the central problems facing all Judaic studies.

Since, for instance, literary criticism is often based on highly subjective criteria and literary studies are so idiosyncratic (particularly when one lacks a tradition of scholarship), he will not be led by copious footnoting to believe that purely objective scholarship really exists. The notion that there is such a thing as objective scholarship is, in itself, an ideological position. The question of taste, constantly the ultimate, vexatious problem for the literary critic, poses difficulties, but opens perspectives. It allows the critic to examine his own tastes. The frequent vagaries of taste are particularly crucial in a literature which produced few works of aesthetic interest before the 1880's; most of the interesting Hebrew matériel was produced in fairly recent times, during eight of the most tumultuous decades in Jewish history. The fluctuations in the literary stock market are bewildering, but sobering. Example: who, today can stomach the hollow bombast of Schneour, one of the most popular poets in modern Hebrew literature? We must account for these shifts in taste since we are usually involved in giving grades, as it were, to authors of various periods.

When personal taste is associated with broader religious social, and political currents we have ideological problems of major proportions. While all scholarship, even the most scrupulously objective, implies a certain ideology, ideological positions—both that of the writer and that of the scholar— in modern Hebrew literature, have assumed, until the past decade, inordinate importance. The critic, after all, is dealing with material written in the recent past, and the issues or anxieties reflected in them are often still alive. On the most obvious level, we confront problems of partisan politics paralleling some of the political positions in Zionist or Israeli politics, but one doesn't have to be too perceptive to detect deeper, more abiding questions which inform many works. Traditional Judaism, for instance, has been treated variously with brazen scorn, pained revulsion, or mawkish sentimentalism. Unless the critic is a pure formalist (as some of the younger Israelis are), or totally insensitive, he must react in some way to the ideological assumptions of much of the material he deals with. (Take, as a glaring example, the attack Avraham Kariv led against Mendele as late as fifteen years ago). In general, modern Hebrew literature has almost unquestioningly adopted and canonized the basic principles of political Zionism. To the extent that we travel through the current post-Zionist era, many of these principles will be questioned. Since the two standard histories of modern Hebrew literature, that of Klausner and Lachower, are clearly based on Zionist assumptions, their inadequacies are becoming more and more obvious. How, finally, does one deal with Holocaust literature which, because of its very subject matter, has been placed in a precinct beyond criticism or scholarship, though it should be clear that there are good and bad books on this theme, too.

The practical implications of these problems of taste and ideology are broadcast in resounding debates every time the literature curriculum of the Israeli gymnasia is up for revision. Who or what should be studied is not merely a matter of aesthetic preference in the Israeli high school, though it is *not* considered legitimate to question whether or not it should be more than a matter of aesthetic preference in the Israeli universities, dedicated, like all universities, to "objective, dispassionate research." In America, the detachment and objectivity of literary scholarship has been severely criticized both by students and younger instructors—as it has been in many other fields. The call to relevance and engagement has been raised in many circles, even in the conservative conferences of the Modern Language Association. While we are all aware of the confusion and hypocrisy attending these arguments, the simple, incontrovertible fact is that the literary establishment and its assumptions have been challenged and must be defended—a process which is fundamentally healthy. All scholarly disciplines can bog down in trivia and an examination of their inner priorities is welcome. In Israel, however, literary criticism has only recently become disengaged from ideological burdens of various types and there is no demand on the part of young critics for a return to engagement. On the contrary: the growing preoccupation with formalism, academically beneficial in itself, is a reflection of the will to be free of ideological burdens.

The opposite position, the total rejection of the claims of objective scholarship in modern Hebrew literature or, for that matter, in any field of Judaic research—and, therefore, teaching—has been one of the obsessive themes in the ideological essays of Baruch Kurzweil, repeated time and again for almost thirty years. These essays have recently been collected in a volume entitled, *Bama'avak al erkhe hayahadut,* and repeatedly attack, as a model of academic vice, the entire lifework of Gershom Scholem. Though Kurzweil's train of argument will not stand critical examination, his main point deserves serious consideration. Under the pretentious, often brutal verbiage, one finds a devastating critique of all of Jewish scholarship (including modern Hebrew literature), in that it is secular, historically oriented, hence ill suited to deal with Judaism, a meta-historical, religious phenomenon. (A similar argument has recently been sounded here in America by "apocalyptic critics" who claim that logical discourse is incapable of dealing with much of contemporary literature which is based on "the aesthetics of silence.") Kurzweil never points to the way out of "the fog of scientistic tranquility" which, he claims, beshrouds Judaic scholarship, but can we, on the other hand, totally ignore the statement: "Judaism as an object of research assumes an acknowledgement of its own undoing"?

Though Kurzweil's basic themes have not changed over the past thirty years, the direction of scholarship and criticism of modern Hebrew literature has. Until 1948, positivistic-historical scholarship was practiced in the university and a vague impressionism in the popular press. During the early 1950's the lectures of Simon Halkin at the Hebrew University, and the essays of Dov Sadan and Baruch Kurzweil opened up a variety of new ways of reading and teaching a literary text. Unfortunately, this change was not accompanied by a rich theoritical literature, with both formal and cultural implications, such as that generated by the New Criticism in America or F. R. Leavis' disciples in England. The sibling relationship between Hebrew and Yiddish literature was slowly acknowledged and it was granted that Hasidic, and not only Haskalah literature, must be regarded as a historical antecedent of modern Hebrew literature. By the early 1960's the New Criticism, which had developed in England and America in the 1930's, was firmly entrenched in Israel and one could sense the first tentative groping towards a more rigorous structuralism based on an international mixture of sources.

Structuralism is the dominant attitude of the quarterly *Ha-Sifrut* (ed. by B. Hrushovski, University of Tel Aviv), first published as recently as Spring 1968, and achieving in an astounding leap the intellectual level of the finest literary journals in any language. I hope that *Ha-Sifrut* is but the first of many scholarly developments for which this field has waited so long. The needs are great: we have few decent monographs on even the major writers, let alone the minor ones; we have no scholarly edition of any modern Hebrew writers; we are lacking many important bibliographies; little has been done in oral documentation though the opportunities have been overwhelming; we need comparative studies of Hebrew and Yiddish, we need regional histories, period histories and, finally, a decent comprehensive history. Most of this work can be done most easily in Israel, with its library and human resource. The American scholar can participate in this work, but he must make relatively frequent trips to Israel to keep abreast of what's going on, and utilize the resources there.

III

Can modern Hebrew literature be taught in an American university? Obviously it can—and is—being taught, although skeptics still doubt it.

My Israeli colleagues are constantly amazed that they have a sprinkling of American students in *their* literature courses; instructors in the American Hebrew Teachers' Colleges often regard this area as their private domain and deny the possibility of its being taught elsewhere—outside of Israel.

The problem is fundamentally one of language acquisition: can an American student learn enough Hebrew to read Bialik or Agnon *sensitively?* Obviously he can, but here again we must confess that most of our undergraduate students have had many years of training before coming to the university and, to this, we often add a year in Israel as a matter of course. Similarly, though French is considerably easier for an American than Hebrew, the number of competent French readers at the B.A. level is shockingly small. Here, too, a year in the natural milieu of the language is imperative. Unfortunately, we still don't have a reasonable first-year college-Hebrew text. An *intelligent* student can reach a good degree of what I call literature-proficiency. Though he has gained this literature-proficiency, he can often take only one full course in modern Hebrew literature in his undergraduate career since the undergraduate major (assuming the student is majoring in the language and literature department) is always a general Hebrew major, in which modern literature is but one sub-area. (I was amazed to discover that the student majoring in modern Hebrew literature at the Hebrew University also spends relatively little time on this area since the requirements in other fields are so exaggerated.) Thus, his knowledge of major writers and works is, indeed, limited though, with proper instruction, particularly with close, sensitive reading of critical texts, he can reach an impressive degree of literary sophistication. The level of instruction, and the quality of literature presented, should always strive to achieve the highest level of work being done in other modern literatures. Thus most of Haskalah literature has little place in an undergraduate course, nor does much of the fiction which is limited to a routine depiction of the *shtetel* or the *kibbutz* without delving into the exciting human drama found in the better authors. The goal is not indoctrination, but the development of sensitivity towards good literature, in general, and good Hebrew literature, in particular. It is not too difficult to arrive at a variety of reasonable curricula for undergraduate courses.

On the graduate level, the design of a curriculum of study is more complex, as would be expected. On the one hand, students arrive with such diverse backgrounds that the professor can hardly find a common denominator. On the other hand, the demands of professional training assume a serviceable foundation in other areas of Judaica, in other modern literatures and, certainly, in Yiddish literature. The director is always torn between what the student really needs and the limits of human ·energy and patience. I am not impressed that the Hebrew University with its years of experience and wide resources, has solved this problem, even in its own terms, let alone in terms which are meaningful to the American graduate school. I designed a program of graduate studies eight years ago and I find that I have revised it upwards every year. In its present state, I could probably not pass it.

We close the circle by returning to the point of our departure, the special relationship this field has with the living *literary* community in Israel. The Israeli institutions, it is quite obvious, have not yet learned how to reproduce themselves in this area and certainly have few instructors to spare for American schools, be they universities, seminaries, or teachers' colleges. The demand for well-trained men is not overwhelming, but it is still substantial. Modern Hebrew literature is taught in at least twenty to thirty undergraduate colleges, four to five graduate schools, in the three major seminaries, and in all the Hebrew colleges; but, since there are only a handful of men seriously engaged in the study of this material, it is inconceivable that all these courses are taught by men professionally committed to the field. Certainly, the academic background of some of the instructors would not lead one to guess that they are versed in the problems of literary criticism or scholarship. In too many instances, an Israeli B.A. in economics or the ability to read *Ha-Doar* are considered qualifications for an instructorship in this area. We arrive at a conclusion which illumines our condition. Modern Hebrew Literature, the discipline most intensely attuned to intellectual life in Israel on so many wavelengths, can utilize Israeli resources and techniques, but must strive to train its own people and create its own academic tradition here if it is to endure in the American academy. And we shall not reach this condition until scholars in other Judaic disciplines stop asking the apocryphal, antiquarian question asked of Yehudah Leb Gordon: "In which century did *you* write?"

TASKS FOR A COMMUNITY OF CONCERN

Leon A. Jick
Brandeis University
Director of the Lown Graduate Center
and Dean of the College

IN American Jewish life the first proposal to establish a faculty of Judaica dates back to 1819. Clearly discussions of the needs and problems of higher Jewish education are quite familiar on the American scene. From the outset the proposers of such faculties and the ultimate teachers of Jewish Studies on the campus have found themselves caught in a dilemma which, as our deliberations have revealed, is still extant. Dealing with materials which had long been regarded as sacred, Judaists found themselves caught in the tension between the existential commitment to a point of view and the intellectual aspiration to scientific detachment. Even those who aspired to objectivity and practiced what they believe to be scientific methodology were frequently governed by *a priori* commitments which affected their choice of subject matter and the conclusions which they reached. Christian critics frequently remained covert apologists for Christianity and subtle denigrators of Judaism. Jewish scholars were not only involved in the problems of Jewish emancipation and survival; they used their scholarly work as a means of bolstering a particular point of view about the nature of that survival in the post-medieval world.

With the passing of decades and the waning of religious and political passions and orthodoxies, the growing integrity in the field of Judaica in all its aspects has brought about a relaxation of tensions. There is no problem in accepting Goodenough as a scholar who revolutionized the understanding of Judaism in late antiquity or Wolfson's contribution to the understanding of church history. Socialists can write about Hassidism with sympathy and understanding: literary critics can deal with both Hebrew and Yiddish literature. Indeed, we have concluded that it is impossible to understand one without the other. Current research transcends the polemical atmosphere which once prevailed in the relationship between what were not only two languages and literatures, but actually two political philosophies and world views.

Despite these changes, tensions persist for us as individuals and for a group like this. Since the problem of individual self-definition has suffused all of our discussions, I shall not comment further on this issue. What must be stressed is the need for us to constitute ourselves as a collectivity and, therefore, to define ourselves as such. Not every so-called scholar of Judaica belongs here; some will not be invited and others will not accept invitations. There are still hostile polemicists who have no place in our midst. The most obvious example is the notorious Trofim Kitchko of the Soviet Union—allegedly a scholar of Judaica but actually an anti-Semitic propagandist. He certainly has no place in our midst. Hebrew is taught in the University of Leningrad but there are no known Jewish students who are studying Hebrew there. Anyone who is involved in such a program has no place here. Of a few teachers of Bible in some fundamentalist Christian seminaries it can still be said that their "Jewish scholarship" is "a spade with which to dig" a grave for Jewish culture and the Jewish people. We need not elaborate on the fact that they do not qualify. At the other extreme we have also acknowledged the fact that scholars in *yeshivot* whose adherence to traditional interpretations must be respected but whose *a priori* commitments severely limit the range of problems or alternatives that they are able to consider, would not find the atmosphere of the secular university and of this kind of group congenial or even tolerable. They, too, have no place. There is a third category which ought to be made welcome but which will eliminate itself. This is the group whose scholarly interests and loyalties are limited to their own tasks and to their own academic disciplines. They will be content to function within various departments —to satisfy their needs for relationships with colleagues in associations of religion, of history, of literature, of sociology or of whatever branch of learning they find congenial to themselves.

What remains is a group devoted to scholarship and to their own intellectual pursuits, but also concerned for a total body of knowledge which is called Judaica or Jewish Studies and, in addition, committed to a special relationship with the community which is the contemporary embodiment of a continuing Jewish civilization. Rejecting the *kapdanut* —the partisanship—of some and the *baishanut*—the detachment—of others, let us constitute ourselves a group which aspires to fulfill scholarly tasks; which employs scientific methodology (insofar as this can be applied to humanistic, historical, and social–scientific materials); which abjures apologetics, but recognizes its relationship to the totality of a culture; which is zealous for enhancing the understanding of this culture as well as for its continuation. Such a group might regard itself as a "community of concern" (if the term had not already been so widely abused in recent times, I would be tempted to use the term *havura)* which can share scholarly problems as they can be shared in no other setting—in the context of the total culture and experience. We must create a forum in which our problems are central and will be considered for their own sake, not merely because of their relationship to any other discipline or their contribution, or lack of contribution, to some other civilization. Finally, we must act in concert to strengthen the contemporary expressions of Judaic culture and to secure the continuity of that culture.

What are the specific tasks, what are the *ma-asim* which are *ikar?* Let me mention but a few: First, I believe that it is the task of such a "community of concern" to provide a forum for regular exchange of ideas among teachers of Judaica and Jewish Studies, and also between teachers and students. I believe that at such forums graduate students, and even interested undergraduates, should be involved in the sharing of scholarly concerns and information. We would be remiss if we did not also acknowledge a responsibility to communicate with those outside the university community, particularly those involved in Jewish education on all levels.

Second, we must provide vehicles for written as well as oral exchange: publications, periodicals, and monographic literature. While publications do exist and interest in certain kinds of monographic literature is growing, the general publishers exercise a nefarious influence in the direction of popularization. All of us are familiar with attempts to dilute scholarly materials so that they become more saleable. We have the responsibility of enlarging the scope of serious periodical and monographic literature.

Third, I believe that we must undertake a review of materials available for teaching of Judaica in colleges and universities. It would be desirable for texts and surveys to be prepared by individuals on their own initiative. Since this is not the case, a serious community of scholars must fill obvious needs and lacks, assuming the leadership in ascertaining that the *lacunae* are filled. More than this: we should not be content until a variety of treatments is available for every serious subject. Jewish scholars are guilty of believing that one book on a subject preempts the field. In no other academic discipline do we accept such a stricture. In every field there is a variety of materials and texts with alternative interpretations and points of view. We must take the initiative in making available diverse approaches to the study of Judaic materials through the publication of texts.

Fourth, a growing need exists for an exchange of ideas and experiences in the organization of Judaica in universities, on the undergraduate as well as on the graduate level. In an informal way such an exchange has taken place at this Colloquium. Many of us have stressed that each experience is distinctive, each university is different; in every instance the local circumstances govern the way in which Judaica functions in a particular setting. Despite the differences there are patterns; there are lessons to be learned from the mistakes that have been made as well as from the successes that have been achieved. What is required is a regular way of exchanging information about norms, patterns, and experiences in both undergraduate and graduate studies. Moreover, we must foster the establishment of consortia cooperative ventures to share resources, to exchange students, faculties, and library facilities. Who, if not the members of a group like this, can set standards for faculty and course offerings in our field?

We have a special responsibility in encouraging graduate studies in Judaica, in supporting graduate students and in assisting in their placement. In anticipation of this Colloquium, I received three calls within two weeks from universities where new Chairs of Judaica were projected. All of these universities indicated that their primary concern was to find men who would fill the positions. Something must be done to facilitate the placement of graduate students, to bring together universities seeking teachers, and graduate students seeking positions.

In addition to helping fill already established positions, we have a commitment to develop the field, to convince universities not simply of the validity but of the importance of Judaic studies, and at the same time to mobilize outside support. The Jewish community must be aroused into taking an interest in university teaching and teachers, into exploring the relationship between university Judaica and related academic endeavors in such places as Hebrew teachers' colleges as well as in pre-collegiate Jewish education.

Finally, I believe that we *do* have another role thrust upon us in clarifying what objective and scholarly teachers can do to strengthen the link between the culture about which they teach and the student community which is the heir of that culture. This last task requires no investments, no publications, no changes in structure, but it perplexes and even frightens us. Professors, after all, do not proselytize and scholars do not solicit. Yet who, if not those immersed in Jewish culture, will demonstrate its validity and its value? Who, if not those with a passion for objective Jewish learning, will serve as models for students, our students, who need to be taught both Torah and in the literal sense *derech eretz?*

A PROPOSAL FOR A
PROFESSIONAL ASSOCIATION

JOSEPH L. BLAU
Columbia University
Professor of Religion

I have been asked to prepare a brief and unprogrammed set of addenda to our colloquy. As you are all aware, without being told, this cannot be of the nature of a summary for one cannot summarize a discussion that has touched on so many fields of both personal and academic concern and that, at times, has verged on group therapy or encounter sessions—even on sensitivity training. What I must try, rather, is to extract from our meetings together something positive that we can carry away from here and on which we can work in the future (and I must say that I think there will be a future, despite some evidence to the contrary that I have heard in the last few days).

Let me begin, since it is traditional to do so, with a parable. In the 1890's, at the then new University of Chicago, a young Canadian student had two favorite teachers, John Dewey and Thorstein Veblen. One day, he went to Dewey's office and found Veblen also there. Inspired by his unexpectedly large audience, this almost beardless youth spoke to his two mentors about his dreams for the future of Canada, the ideals in terms of which he hoped to build his own life significantly into those dreams, his visions of his own greatness. He asked his teachers only the question: "How do I get started?" or, if I may translate, how can I turn my vision into a program? As one man, Dewey and Veblen replied, "Get yourself an organization." The young man, happily, was able to follow this prescription, and the name of Mackenzie King resounds in Canadian history.

We, too, have visions, dreams, ideals. There is, I suspect, a far greater area of common agreement among us than the casual auditor might suspect. After all, one does not argue with a Fascist about subtle shades of meaning in the term "democracy." This one argues with a fellow believer in democracy, often carrying on the argument with enough virulence to suggest to the Fascist that one of us (though he is not sure which) may be on his side. Our goal might be stated in broadest terms as, to make a place in American higher education for the studies in the life, thought, and culture of Jews, past and present, not only as a means of stimulating the enrichment of educational content now, and as a factor in Jewish survival in time to come, but also because we are convinced that these studies have an intrinsic value that is like and yet unlike comparable studies of other ethnic groups. Each of us might put his own chief stress on one of these phrases; we would all, I think, accept the whole statement. I think, too, that we are agreed, in principle, that the standard of intellectual rigor and clarity of statement to which we implicitly subscribe when we call for the incorporation of Jewish studies into higher education is that of academe, though each of us recognizes (in others, if not in himself) that performance invariably falls below the standard we set for ourselves, for we are men, not gods.

How to turn this vision into a program? The answer is still, as it was to Mackenzie King nearly eighty years ago, "Get yourself an organization." Let us begin to move, before we leave these hospitable grounds, toward the formation of an association for Jewish studies that will be both scholarly and professional in its aims and in its work. I shall not say much about the scholarly side; it has entered into our previous discussions, and properly so, for each of us is, in his own way and within limits that his colleagues are only too happy to point out, a scholar. Scholarship nourishes our personal life and, for some of us, defines our personal faith. An organization that did not contribute to our scholarly growth would be to us merely a labor union and, as such, not our concern. But an organization solely dedicated to the furtherance of our scholarly aims would not do, either. For we are members of a special branch of a profession that is ancient and still not without honor. I confess here that, since my remote high-school days nearly fifty years ago, I have been thrilled by academic processions as by no other parades, by academic regalia as by no other costume—that to this day I never put on my robes without a recognition that I have earned a place in a noble guild whose roots go back into the past and whose fruits will continue to appear while there are men on earth—that I speak a silent prayer that I may never, in word or deed, bring anything but respect to this profession that has given me so much. And I feel, and hope you feel, too, that these gifts obligate me to serve whatever, in my limited wisdom, I conceive to be in the best interests of that profession. Since I conceive it to be in the best interests of the profession to which I am proud to belong to work for the inclusion of Jewish studies in higher education, I have the obligation to contribute of my time and talents and energy, over and above my scholarly contributions, over and above my work with students, in and out of the classroom, to the too often tedious managerial, political, social, even economic tasks that I have lumped under the term "professional."

I do not think we should leave here with an association born, full-grown, out of the froth and spume of our meeting. Our colloquium has had an emotional impact on us all, and I distrust actions taken on the tide of emotion. I think, rather, that we should leave with an agreement to meet again—here, if our hosts will be so kind, and when there is no hurricane in the offing—to debate in calm and tranquility the desirability and the precise nature of the association of which I have been speaking. In order that there may be a formulation on the basis of which your private reflections may be carried on, and possibly as a guide to at least part of the agenda of that future meeting—I have set down the following statement, copies of which you will all receive:

> Be it resolved: that the scholars here assembled do constitute themselves as the initial membership to establish the American Association for Jewish Studies, whose object shall be to promote, maintain, and improve the teaching of Jewish Studies in American colleges and universities by:
>
> 1. Providing occasions for both regional and national meetings for the exchange of ideas and information;
> 2. Publishing a newsletter for the rapid diffusion of new materials and news of work in progress; possibly adding to this, as conditions warrant, a journal for the careful and thorough presentation of scholarly materials;
> 3. Stimulating the building of library holdings in Jewish Studies wherever possible and devising means for informing all professors of Jewish Studies of the new acquisitions; stimulating also programs of scholarly reprints and translations;
> 4. Setting advisory minimal standards for:
>   a. survey courses in Jewish Studies
>   b. undergraduate major programs
>   c. graduate programs
>   d. Jewish-studies elements in interdepartmental programs and by offering advisory services to colleges and universities beginning or expanding their programs in Jewish Studies;
> 5. Speaking as the collective voice of its members within the total academic community in North America, whenever such a united representation shall be needed;

6. Establishing and maintaining a register of qualified scholars in the area of Jewish Studies, in order to serve as a responsible agency for placement, matching the candidates and the openings as precisely as possible and reducing the possibility of the appointment of unqualified persons;

7. Developing techniques and sources of information for identifying potential recruits to the field as early as feasible in their educational development and in other ways, working to increase and improve manpower in the field;

8. Cooperating with other academic professional organizations for specific *ad hoc* goals of academic life as the occasion may arise;

9. Serving as an agency to publicize, both in the general and in the Jewish communities, the work that is being done in the field of Jewish Studies to the end that further financial and moral support may be given to our work on the basis of results already achieved, rather than presenting a claim as of right

10. Cooperating with centers of academic Jewish Studies in Israel and other nations in developing plans and programs for the most effective use of the scattered resources of Jewish Studies.

I have said that we should not move too fast. In concluding, let me only add that we should not move too slowly, either. "There is a tide in the affairs of men"—let us not miss the floodcrest.

A NOTE ON ESTABLISHING CHAIRS
OF JEWISH STUDIES

HARVIE BRANSCOMB
Chancellor Emeritus
Vanderbilt University

THE Editor of the proceedings of the Colloquium has kindly invited me to contribute a statement on the general topic of establishing Chairs of Jewish Studies in American universities. There are others who could do this with much more knowledge than I can claim, notably the officers and moving spirits of that remarkable and effective organization, the B'nai B'rith Hillel Foundation. My only qualification for expertise in the topic is that I was responsible in some part for initiating Chairs in two private universities, Duke University and Vanderbilt University. Both are in the South, both institutions maintained schools for the training of Protestant clergy, both were reasonably conservative institutions. My experience, in other words, is limited to initiating such studies in what might have been called at the time WASP universities, though both no doubt would have resented the title.

The Duke Chair was established in 1943, the Vanderbilt one, in 1949. In the former instance my relationship was as a member of the faculty and, for a short while, as dean; at Vanderbilt I was the chief administrative officer. This latter situation had only one advantage, that one could move somewhat more expeditiously when one made recommendations to one's self. The basic problems, however, were the same—to plan programs that were useful and desirable, to persuade various groups that this was so, to determine the proper academic setting and relationship for the program and, as always, to arrange the financing.

The first question which one had to answer was, Why do it? What are you trying to accomplish? The question was sincere—it did not arise from hostility or suspicion, but rather from puzzlement. The real answer was in terms of certain general considerations with which some of us had lived since our graduate-school days. To graduate students of Christian origins and comparative ethics in the 1920's it was already clear that the picture of Judaism in the first century A.D., and of the relation of the Christian movement to it held by most Christians, was simply not true.

This article, and the succeeding one by Professor Sandmel, were written for this publication, and were not delivered at the Colloquium.

Rabbinic materials had begun to become available to nonrabbinic scholars, and even such efforts as those of Strack and Billerbeck to interpret the data in the conventional manner could not disguise the fact that early Christianity had taken from its heritage far more than it had rejected. What had happened was perhaps inevitable—the seceding body had been chiefly involved in criticism of the parent religious faith, while common convictions and affirmations were taken for granted. This negative posture, in due course, became enshrined in the sacred literature and thus became orthodoxy for succeeding centuries. Perhaps a similar response occurred on the other side—painful events do not encourage objectivity—but for Judaism the struggle for survival was to be paramount and events in connection with the birth of Christianity received less attention. The drama of origins is always more important to a new social body than are the same events seen only as part of a long and traumatic history.

If these historical misunderstandings could be cleared up, we believed, the doors would be opened to a redefinition of relationships and cooperation in matters of common interest, both scholarly and practical. This particular concern was of course only part of a larger problem: the almost universal popular ignorance as to the tenets and social principles of Judaism. To the average person, Jewish thought and practice was a body of esoteric lore to be interpreted as one wished. The interfaith movement, for all of its goodwill, was bound to be superficial until it could rest on greater knowledge of the actual content of the faith with which one was urged to cooperate. All of this was clearly a job for the universities, particularly for those which maintained divinity schools or other special programs for the study of religion.

To these simple ideas—which were more true a quarter of a century ago than today—we added a third argument. Duke had required its undergraduates to take one course in religion, which meant, in practice, in the Christian religion. The requirement had been relaxed but rules of graduation were such as to encourage exposure to at least one course in the Department. Jewish students were excused from this requirement, but this placed the administration in an awkward position if, that is, one defended the requirement. One was reminded of the medieval attitude which permitted Jewish moneylenders to carry on their useful but ecclesiastically banned activity on the ground that they were going to be damned anyhow. If the requirement was sound in principle, we argued, a course should be provided for these students in their own faith.

These considerations determined, from the outset, the course selection for a proposed appointment in this field. Since we were talking of one man only, he would hardly have a department of his own. An appointment to the Department of Religion in the Graduate School and College was proposed, but it was suggested that the appointee be located in an office in the Divinity School building. A course on Judaism in the First Century A.D., opened to graduate students and Divinity School students, and an undergraduate course on Contemporary Judaism, were to be the primary teaching duties. In addition, it was hoped that the individual chosen might contribute by his own studies to the further clarification of historical and other problems in the field of Judaeo-Christian history. The emphasis in this proposal thus fell primarily—perhaps unduly so—on what George Foot Moore called "normative Judaism."

It was obvious that much of the success or failure of this undertaking would depend upon the personal qualities of the individual appointed. In the first place, we had to find some one willing to take the job, willing to work, that is, in a not unfriendly but nevertheless alien religious environment. He must be interested in the problem of communication across frontiers too often closed. He should be a person of outgoing temperament who would enjoy contact with Christian scholars and invite friendships in turn. Without question he must be a good scholar. And finally, he must be a loyal representative of his faith. This last was based on the belief that to correct inveterate misunderstandings and prejudices it was important to convey not only the literary and historical facts but the ethos of the Jewish faith as well, its spiritual meaning to its adherents.

Finally there was the financial problem. The University took the familiar position that with the many requests before it, it could not provide the funds necessary for this new venture. At this point the Hillel Foundation was approached. It agreed to finance the chair initially. We then secured for the appointment Dr. John Goldin, an attractive young Jewish scholar, who was given the title, Lecturer in Jewish Literature and Thought.

The undertaking proved successful on a limited scale. Dr. Goldin was a lucid and persuasive teacher. He was liked by his colleagues. Most members of the University faculty were pleased at broadening the curriculum in religion. The Jewish undergraduates were gratified that their special interests had been recognized, though a curious reluctance to take the course was observed. But several problems developed. There were few Jewish scholars on the University faculty at that time—the University had emerged from its college cocoon less than a decade before

—and Durham was a small industrial town in which the local Jewish community was neither large enough nor rich enough in cultural resources to offer much to the newcomer and his family in terms of social life. A small detail also complicated matters. Dr. Goldin was liberal in scholarship and theology, but strict in regards to the dietary laws. This caused an awkward situation on several occasions. More importantly, the dietary matter created some difficulty in regard to social contacts in homes. Our scholar, I fear, felt himself a little isolated. These matters, however, would very probably have been overcome with time and growing friendships, but for one basic issue which had not been resolved. Since the University had declined to commit itself to maintaining the appointment, tenure was uncertain and insecure and, without this, advancement in rank was largely meaningless. When two years later opportunities elsewhere came to Dr. Goldin, he resigned the post. In the absence of firm financial commitments by the University the appointment was allowed to lapse.

A start, however, had been made, and Duke had the distinction of being the first university in the South, I believe, to introduce Jewish Studies through a full-time appointment. The courses had proven interesting to students of both faiths, the faculty had approved the inclusion of Jewish Studies in the curriculum, and no problems of relationships had been encountered. A few years later the University reconsidered the matter, placed the necessary funds in its regular budget, and appointed to its College faculty a scholar trained in the field. Dr. Goldin can feel satisfied with the foundation which he laid.

The establishment of Jewish Studies at Vanderbilt came several years later. The same general considerations which had underlain the program at Duke again were applicable and, in fact, even more pressing in that the Duke program had been dropped. There was however one important difference. Nashville was an older and larger city than Durham, and the Jewish community was—and is—one of the city's greatest assets. It is a highly cultured group, and it welcomed the idea of a university program in the field of Jewish history and thought, and gave it moral and financial support. The representative of the program was thus assured of a constituency of his own, and was provided from the outset with special funds for library acquisitions, travel, and other desirable expenditures. The Board of Trust of the University approved and encouraged the proposal when it was presented to it. Finances were provided again by a grant from the Hillel Foundation, by annual contributions from the local community, and by some funds from the University. The program thus was a cooperative one, with the University's share of the cost increasing over the years. In appreciation of the assistance which had been rendered and of the national service of the organization, the University named the chair the Hillel Professorship of Jewish Literature and Thought. It was the good fortune of the University to secure as its first occupant Dr. Samuel Sandmel, who brought to it the combination of sound academic training, a warm and engaging personality, a scholarly interest in the problem of Christian origins, and marked effectiveness as a teacher. Under his leadership the chair was well established and while most of Sandmel's writings came after his transfer to a major institution of his own faith, the program can claim some credit for his important contributions to the understanding of Christian origins by means of Jewish scholarship. After his resignation Dr. Lou Silberman successfully carried on the program. It has been useful to students, enriching to the University and to the Nashville community, has contributed to scholarship, and has been influential with other institutions.

These experiences perhaps are not representative on a national scale but they may provide some guidelines for similar undertakings by institutions of moderate size. In reflecting on the experience the following general comments seem appropriate. Perhaps they may serve as guidelines for similar undertakings:

1. Provision for the study of Jewish history and thought is a proper and rewarding university function.
2. If undertaken, stability for the program, and status and tenure for the individual appointed is essential.
3. If a theological or divinity school exists on the campus close relationship to this faculty should be provided, but a separate and independent status is desirable.
4. It is highly useful to involve the local community, more especially the local Jewish community, in the planning and its implementation.
5. In most institutions the teaching function will be the primary one, with large-scale research and doctoral development left to other institutions.
6. In selecting an individual to initiate such a program personal qualities are equally as important as scholarship. Tact and a sense of humor have high priority in the job description.
7. The program must have administrative support, but will have to win its own way. It should not be pushed, promoted or overly publicized.

SCHOLAR OR APOLOGIST?

SAMUEL SANDMEL
*Professor of Bible
and Hebrew Literature
Hebrew Union College—Jewish Institute of Religion
Cincinnati, Ohio*

DAVID HOFFMANN, the eminent German scholar, in an essay written as I recall it, in the 1890's—the essay does not readily come back to hand—lamented that in all Germany there was not a single chair of Judaica. In his context there was the implication that chairs in Judaica could, in an academic way, meet distortion which he alleged existed in the scholarly description of Judaism on the part of German New Testament scholars. To this we will return.

Again, in the early 1940's and before the United States became involved in World War II, Harvie Branscomb, then a professor at Duke University, became deeply interested in establishing a chair of Jewish Studies. After the end of World War II, by which time he had become chancellor at Vanderbilt University, he appointed me to a chair in Jewish Literature and Thought. For that Duke appointment I can say in all modesty he was interested in me, personally. The necessary funds were assembled; by then, however, I had filed papers to become a chaplain in the Navy, so that I was not eligible. Naturally, he turned elsewhere, and interviewed a number of possible appointees. In speaking to one of these, and stressing the pioneer nature of the proposed chair and hence the desire that the appointee be somewhat elastic, Dr. Branscomb was a bit startled to hear the man say that, although he was Jewish, Judaism meant very little to him. I was in the Navy by then; Dr. Branscomb wrote to me saying that he was interested only in a practicing Jew, not in an ex-Jew. To this, too, we will return.

Is it reasonable, or even realistic, to conclude that there is a difference, at least in degree, and possibly in kind, between chairs of Jewish Studies and other chairs? Certainly in the case of other chairs most, perhaps all of us, would assert strongly that the personal dispositions, or prepossessions, or religious affiliation of a possible incumbent should never enter

103

into an evaluation of the prospective candidate for the position. Would we hold this to be the case in a chair in Judaica? Would we be acquiescent, if we were consulted, to the appointment of a qualified Gentile or Christian, were one available?

At Duke, when my appointment was contemplated, it was on the basis that it would take place at that future point at which I would have completed my Ph.D. work. Indeed, the Ph.D. was tacitly assumed to be the appropriate and necessary set of credentials, as it is in most appointments in universities. Not that my rabbinic training was scorned; on the contrary. It was simply assumed that a rabbinic training was broad, rather than specialized, and comprehensive, but not fully disciplined. I have no recollection of anyone's saying that a Ph.D. was, by implication, a scholar and a rabbi, an apologist. But certainly, especially if we go beyond the Jewish scene, there is a broad assumption that ministers and priests (and rabbis) who do not have the Ph.D. are apologists, and that Ph.D.'s are not necessarily so.

To revert now to the two opening statements, Hoffmann's lament about the absence of Jewish chairs implied that such chairs would serve an apologetic purpose, and Branscomb's wish for the incumbent to be a practicing Jew implies, at the minimum, that the incumbent would be a Jewish spokesman in some way. How can these two opinions be reconciled with the supposition of the academic world that a scholar is, relatively, objective, dispassionate, and—above all—committed to the impartial search for the truth and not to some antecedent convictions?

On at least three fronts there are situations which exist, and have existed, which by their very nature tend to blur the otherwise clear distinction between the scholar and the apologist. Two of these I have experienced, but the third is of an origin, so recent, that I know about it only at second or third hand.

The first of these I will here denominate as endemic, popular anti-Semitism. This sort of thing in the American scene, especially around universities, is as sporadic as it is vague. Its focus is on Jews, rather than on Judaism. Its form is diverse. At times it is little more than the product of the enduring vestiges of the campus social divisions, with the yield of Gentile fraternities on the one hand, and Jewish on the other. (Most of us with campus experience are led to wonder just what it is in Jewish fraternities that entitles them to be called Jewish!) Some incident, of no great consequence, can arise in this dormitory, or that, and some knowledge of it comes to the Hillel director or the professor of Jewish Studies, or both. Or, adjacent to the campus there is a place from which the routine anti-Semitic publications (such as *The Protocols of the Elders of Zion)* may circulate.

By and large such anti-Semitism is of little direct concern to the Professor of Jewish Studies. Not only are the faculty and administration of the university squarely against such things, but the student body is also against it. Ocassionally the administration may want the counsel of the Jewish professor on the best way that it should try to handle a particular matter. But, by and large, this sort of thing is in the domain of the university authorities, not of the Jewish professor. Only when some single incident gets out of hand (I have never experienced this) or threatens to (this I have experienced) need a Jewish professor become involved. Indeed, in terms of "strategy," there are so many people, advantageously placed, who can deal with such matters, that the Jewish professor can, with clear conscience, abstain from direct intervention and, certainly, he can abstain from highly visible intervention.

The second area is directed not against Jews but against Judaism. Its manifestation, as I shall suggest, can be diverse. Its remote (and in some cases, proximate) source is Christianity. Its form is genteel, not uncouth. There is a Christian conviction that Christianity, historically, emerged into history as a better and finer thing than Judaism. (I have elsewhere written about this at some length.) Derivative from this conviction is a range of views, some ancient, some modern. One can encounter some modern adaptations of the ancient view that Christianity supplanted Judaism in God's favor, and that such supplanting proceeded to a point at which Jews became (and are) a rejected people. Especially outside the faculty of religion, one can hear, or read, the words of eminent professors, who are personally free of deliberate malice, that Judaism was, and is, a narrow, exclusive tribalism, and Christianity a great universal religion. A typical opinion (again from outside the faculty of religion) is the judgment that Jews worshiped a cruel and vindictive God, while Christians worshiped a God of love. I do not think it is necessary to multiply examples of this sort of thing, on the part of professors whose knowledge of both Judaism and of Christianity is superficial. This kind of thing is innately part of that world which has been dominantly Christian for so many centuries. It is a view that can emerge even from a professor of intellectual history, who denies the historical reliability of the Gospels, and the divinity or special role of Jesus, but still seems to believe, or to feel, that the Gospel portrait of Judaism was, and is, reliable. Such people have never heard of Travers Herford or of George Foot Moore, and one despairs of our ever reaching the point at which the

favorable results of modern (even Christian) scholarship will ever make
some impact. The tragedy here is that such inaccurate things are spoken
or written by men of genuine good will, who would selflessly combat
overt anti-Semitism. These people are free of malice; their trespass is
either insufficient information or some inability to absorb the scanty
information which they have.

A distortion of Judaism is often reflected by "secularists," whose
anti-religion is normally anti-Christian, and whose anti-Judaism is only
coincidental. The premise which prevails is that every manifestation of
religion is, and has been, bad, as the historical record of wars and
persecutions clearly shows and, since the major facet of that vague
entity Judaism was and is religion, Judaism is subsumed likewise under
what is bad. Two major items seem to me the most frequently cited: one,
the perpetual exclusivism of Jews and, second, curiously enough, the
excommunication of Spinoza. Such distortions normally are the result
of exasperating half-truths, not of total falsity. But not only are there
these half-truths, but counterbalancing or corrective data are either
unpresented or else are totally unknown. Indeed, the dispensers of these
distorting half-truths are very often professors who are themselves Jews
and, in some cases, Jews who are synagogue members and in their own
ways loyal to some array of Jewish causes.

I have, up to this point, exempted departments of religion from consideration. I should begin by asserting that chairs in Judaica have
normally been created because of the genuine appreciation of Judaism
by such scholars. Not only do such people defend Jews and Judaism, but
they have an affirmative solicitude for them. In general, such people
will contend against the Gospel portrayal of Judaism, and they will
emphasize the Jewishness of Jesus, and insist that the criticisms attributed
in the Gospels to Jesus must be understood as an internal Jewish matter
of Jesus criticizing, from within, the Judaism to which he was personally
loyal. Such scholars will insist on the parity of Judaism in the scheme
of academic disciplines. Such scholars, often enough personally devout
Christians, are the legatees of a Christian scholarship which is not only
honest and critical, but often even iconoclastic. Uninhibited in their
strictures against Christian tradition, they lean over backward to exempt
Judaism from such strictures. I have personally never encountered more
wholesome or more admirable people than Christian academicians in the
field of religion. I have seen how they struggle against the tone of German
New Testament scholarship, with its abiding disparagement of Judaism.
I know how many of them struggle against that description of Judaism

(which bothered David Hoffmann) as only a dry and arid legalism. To generalize, and thus to overlook a mere handful of glaring individual examples to the contrary, these people are our friends and our defenders.

As to distortions, let there be no mistaking a fact of life. The accumulated Christian scholarship has a tone of anti-Judaism. In the United States and Britain, Christian scholars have struggled valiantly to rid scholarship of this marring, anti-Jewish tone. While a number of great names can be cited, none seems to me equal to that of George Foot Moore. In his essay, "Christian Writers on Judaism,"* he set forth a bill of particulars respecting what, to his mind, were the distortions and inadequacies in the eminent Christian scholars of the nineteenth century. Moore, and those whom he influenced (among them Harvie Branscomb), greatly altered the tone of Christian scholarship on Judaism; this, one can see by comparing a book in English on New Testament written before and after the publication of Moore's *Judaism* (1924). Moore's impact on German scholarship has winnowed out most of the snide derogations of Jews; it has scarcely touched, however, the denigration of Judaism. Continental scholars have told me that in many a German seminary, the snide has been lifted out of the classroom and transferred to the refectory or the corridor, and there it persists.

There is, then, in the arena of public academic notice a legacy of Christian academic denigration of Judaism. What is the Jewish scholar to do about this? I know of no better procedure than that of Moore and his disciples, namely, to challenge the distortions in an academic way, and to provide a more responsible, more accurate sholarship than that possessed by the deliberate or unconscious distorters. The apologist is the scholarship, not the scholar.

A complexity exists, though, which the Jewish scholar needs to recognize, but often seems to me not to. I can perhaps best illustrate this by drawing a distinction, which I consider to be valid, between a Julius Wellhausen and a Harnack on the one hand, and Paul de Lagarde and Bruno Bauer on the other. These latter two were *personally* vicious Jew-haters, and Bruno Bauer fought against German Jews acquiring the basic rights of German citizenship. Wellhausen and Harnack, on the other hand, were modern critical scholars whose studies in Christian disciplines were as iconoclastic as were their attitudes to Bible (Old Testament) or to New Testament. If their work contains disparagement of Judaism, it also contains equal disparagement of Christianity. To

*In, *Harvard Theological Review,* 1921.

convict them (usually without a trial) of deliberate anti-Semitism is, in context, at least a little far-fetched; it is easier, and only after a trial, to convict them of bondage to schematization (i.e., the "evolution" of all religions, and of nineteenth-century oversimplification) than of focused anti-Semitism. Again, one meets this challenge in an academic manner.

But, to move now from the direct matter of the inadequate academic portrayal of Judaism, there is at hand a much more subtle matter which is a reality. It is not a difficulty in persons as much as in situation, and exists in those Christians who criticize Wellhausen and Harnack; it is even in those who protest honestly and vigorously against the distortion of Judaism. Nevertheless, there are those who, direct or indirect legatees of Paul, see 'the realm of religion as one in which the spirit is constantly at war with the letter, and the axiom with which they approach matters is that the spirit is good, and the letter (whether in traditional Christianity or in Judaism) is bad. Relatively free of the German disparagement of Jewish legalism and even determined to be fair to it, they are nevertheless hostile to legalism. It is in such terms that the Christian adulation of Martin Buber is to be explained, for he appears in such Christian eyes to be that authentic Jew who has risen beyond Jewish legalism into the realm of the spirit. There is often an unconscious setting of Buber over and against Judaism.

Now, as I see it, Judaism is not, and never was merely a legalism, and as I see it, the contrast between spirit and letter is a false one for the simple reason that, in Judaism, there always has been such a thing as the spirit of the letter. The question here—and I am restating this—is not that of the shabby distortions of which New Testament scholarship had been guilty, or of gross academic error, but, more subtly, the issue of the congruency of Judaism at its authentic best with the needs and requirements of religion in our time and in the future. Such Christians, however deeply rooted they are in Christianity, are not as rooted as we Jews are in the historical Jewish community, with the result that their ties are not like ours, nor their restraints like ours. As it were, they *as Christians* become advocates of something with little or no clear Christian precedent whereas we are, by virtue of our credentials, competent in a tradition which is preeminently an accumulation of the past. There are, of course, Christian antiquarians. But acute and creative minds in the Christian faculty, quite apart from these antiquarians, are dealing, or trying to deal, with universal man in the future. Sometimes a friendly outsider like me has wondered how much beyond lip service to historical Christianity informs these efforts. The fact seems to me to be that many such people are not concerned with even lip service.

If I have been tolerably clear, then the Jewish scholar exists in a context in which, at the one extreme, the academic disparagement of Judaism manages to persist; at the other extreme, this in an atmosphere of friendliness, the Jewish scholar is a spokesman for a rich but past tradition, a particular tradition, kindred to ancient Greek or Roman culture, while the Christian includes the man exploring the unlimited future of man. Is there not all the difference in the world between the Jewish scholar who, in a facet of his work, argues for the congruency of Judaism with the modern age or the future, and the Christian philosopher, theologian, or sociologist, whose preoccupation is with an age to come? That is to say, the tacit assumption prevails that our Jewish scholarship is oriented to past glories, and theirs to the future grandeur of man.

What about this vision of man's future? Ordinarily the faculty in religion outnumbers the Jews—usually it is the Jew, not the Jews—so that there does not exist in one and the same person the potential dual responsibility of depth in past scholarship and a venturing into the future. Indeed, that academic type which is the meticulous student of the past or the present may by temperament be unsuited to venturesomeness about the future. But I am troubled by the implication that can be drawn from such situations, that the vistas of Judaism are limited to what has been, and those of Christianity to what may or will be. I cannot escape the uneasy feeling that there is an assumption of a built-in limit to our effectiveness even if, as scholars and teachers of the past, we are unlimitedly effective. Unless we can muster the ability, too, to speak from a Jewish perspective about a universal future we are abdicating a crucial responsibility.

The supreme issue is not whether past Christian scholars have distorted Judaism (as some have), but whether, in the context of the university, even the most wholesome fairness to past Judaism may not eventuate in unconscious and implicit distortion. It seems to me that here we are not victims of some unfairness, but rather victims of limited horizons. Surely our approach to Judaism must be, in addition to academic, intellectual (and not folksy); it must be an exposition of ideas (and not merely our ceremonies); it must be a challenge in the realm of the mind (not simply spoken or literary Hebrew). There is a challenge to us which far transcends our academic prowess.

Surely the introduction of chairs of Judaica, the most significant development in modern American Judaism, is only a first step. Judaica departments need, and will increasingly need, broadening. A Judaism department will need a concern for the future—both the Jewish and the universal—as urgently as it needs the specialists in the subjects of ages gone by.

The third area I have not personally experienced, not as a professor resident on a campus. I have experienced it in visits as a lecturer, and only in the mildest form. I have in mind the State of Israel.

My own experience is limited to what I could describe as disinterested questioning, namely, why a State of Israel? why such an outpouring of Jewish feeling about it? and the question, Will affairs in the Middle East ever be settled?

When I was a graduate student at Yale, I was not personally involved in an incident. A Yale professor wrote an anti-Zionist book—a mild, partisan, and, so I thought, a silly book. Zionists in New Haven protested *to the university*. There were those in New Haven who wanted to do even more, but they were persuaded that the particular matter could be given undue importance by their contemplated actions; also they were reminded of the matter of academic freedom, even for those whose sentiments others disapprove of. This incident scarcely amounted to more than a ripple.

If I understand rightly, today anti-Israel sentiments are held by a good many professors, and openly expressed by a large fraction of their number. Moreover, the "new left" is hostile to Israel; and many a campus has an active and articulate Arab enclave, which carries on a variety of activities, including the raising of funds for El-Fatah.

Surely this situation is one in which the professor of Judaica can scarcely remain entirely on the sidelines. Indeed, for him to do so is, to my mind, scarcely to be applauded.

I know of no formula to suggest. It is vapid to propose that the Jewish scholar maintain his dispassionate role, for the reality is that, for better or worse, he is "involved." Perhaps the issue can be this, in what form and in what strategy does he channel his personal involvement? In general, it is perhaps an error in strategy for him to abandon completely his role as a scholar (bearing in mind the events of this past December when "radicals" tried to force the American Historical Association to become aligned with "involvement"); perhaps his effectiveness in the long run is jeopardized by his responses to an *ad hoc* situation. Or perhaps he can readily justify his doing absolutely nothing on the grounds of wishing to forfend against jeopardizing his academic reputation by doing something. I must confess that my thinking is very clouded on this matter, this, because of my prejudice that the professor of Jewish Studies is an academician, not an activist; I see his role as that of a theoretician, not as that of one who deals with concrete, tangible affairs. My thinking is the more clouded by my resentment that the situation has arisen in which this dilemma exists, for I should have preferred that it had not arisen.

Is it possible (or if possible, desirable) for one and the same person to be both the detached scholar and the involved citizen? I do not know. The things which I would tend to advocate seem to me to be reflections of my own personal disposition, rather than a thought-through intellectual position. Thus, calmness rather than hot-headedness seems to me desirable. Again, I have the conviction that, in the academic scene, the more urgent a divisive matter is, the more urgent are courtesy, civility, and genteelness. I tell myself that, in the long run, these qualities persuade a campus community more tellingly than do discourtesy and denunciation.

Groping, as is evident from these words of mine, I suppose that ultimately the matter seems to me to be this: that it is academic competency that brings a man to an academic integrity. If and when he becomes personally involved, it is in the framework of a persistent adherence to academic values. Others may trespass in this regard; he should not.

In sum, the apologetics ought to remain that of the values in Judaism, and not the eloquence, or the tact, or the skills of the particular professor. David Hoffmann did not want academic chairs so that Jewish persons would confront a distorting scholarship, but so that the truth could confront it. Branscomb did not want a disembodied Judaism, but an authentic, full-bodied Judaism represented within the total university. We, ourselves, when we can manage the situation, ought never be apologists in our persons; it is our scholarship which should be our apologetics.

SCHOLARSHIP AND CONTINUITY: DILEMMA AND DIALECTIC

IRVING GREENBERG
Yeshiva University
Associate Professor of History;
Rabbi, Riverdale Jewish Center

IN May 1818 Leopold Zunz published his call for the scientific study of Jewish creativity to take its place with the great surge in scientific study of universal culture(s).[1] Gerson Cohen has correctly pointed out that Zunz's dreams for achievements in research have been more than surpassed and, were he alive today and judging by his explicit statements on needed research in the essay "On Rabbinic Literature," "he would probably be ecstatic with joy."[2] But, of course, there were at least two other motives behind Zunz's scholarly concerns. One was his fear or conviction that the rapid assimilation of Jews was "carrying post-Biblical Hebrew literature to its grave." Wissenschaft therefore must record and preserve this literature before it disappears. (Preserve used in the sense of preserving butterflies in formaldehyde.) The second motive was Zunz's "conviction that only a scientific approach to the Jewish past can result in a fair estimate of the nature of Judaism and the Jew."[3] The value of this fair estimate would be, therefore, greater appreciation and acceptance of contemporary Jews as well as post-Jewish culture. It would undergird intelligent efforts at political and religious reform, making it possible "to know and distinguish the old which is still of use, the antiquated which has become pernicious and the new which is desirable."[4]

We can agree that the Wissenschaft des Judentums movement was marked by a new objectivity of approach to the tradition, a willingness to see it from the outside as an object of research, yielding its monolithic structure and its functions as "norm for our judgments." We can agree that modern Jewish Studies in the university setting have extended and surpassed the first goal, not least by locating these studies in a far more open, universal medium than Jewish scholarship has functioned in up to now. Thus Gershon Scholem's critique of his predecessors and thrust for even less value-centrism and parochialism in Jewish scholarship is also

115

continually being realized.[5] But what of Zunz's other goals? The goal of preservation appears, in the light of history, to have been premature. Neither post-Biblical Hebrew literature nor Jewish culture generally has been "carried to its grave." Neither assimilation nor holocaust has "closed" Jewish history.[6] On the other hand, the goal of Wissenschaft playing a role in adapting Judaism and Jews to the newly emerged world culture would appear to be more promising and necessary than ever. It is a dimension which Zunz's contemporary successors must also confront.

It is a truism that the Wissenschaft des Judentums movement was a response to the modernization crisis of Jewry. It sought, consciously or unconsciously, greater respectability for Judaism and Jews (respectability defined as being more respected or more studied by Western methods and norms.) Its practitioners—East or West—whether positively directed or ambivalent to the ongoing value of the tradition—or even while weighing conversion!—felt some call and concern for the continuation of Judaism. Then, immediate and urgent as is the desire to further strengthen, direct and restore wholeness to the scholarship dimension of the movement, the question of assimilation and continuity remains and emerges with even greater intensity for reasons I will delineate below.

The recent creation of the American Association for Jewish Studies reflects a recognition that more is at stake in Jewish Studies than increasing research and teaching efforts in the field. Such a recognition was tacitly conceded in the fact that it was Jewish practitioners of Jewish Studies who were invited to its founding conference. Nor is this field unique or pioneering in recognizing the potential involvement in or responsibility for societal concerns by scholarship. This insight, spurred by student and young scholars' activism, is somewhere between a revolution, a fad, a professional collapse and/or a "failure of nerve" on American campuses today. The fact that it is slower in coming to the Jewish field is probably a function of the relatively lesser interest of Jewish students and the Jewish community in Jewish Studies; of the fact that Jews are still more dominated by the urge to make it than to shake it in American life; and by the recent and rapid expansion of Jewish Studies on campuses. This last means that many old-time practitioners are living and rooted in more passive cultural settings and the newer ones are in an expansionary and upwardly mobile phase which tends to undermine activism by occupying its potential energies elsewhere. However, the problems of Jewish identity and Jewish survival are bound to emerge and haunt Judaic scholars with greater intensity. This is because the crisis of modernization is entering a new level of intensity in the Jewish community.

The social and economic absorption of Jews into the mainstream of modern life and the achievement of its rewards is now all but complete. American Jewry is almost ninety percent located in or about the large urban centers (over 250,000 population) in middle- and upper-middle-class neighborhoods. It is peculiarly and increasingly in professional and occupational strata where modernization and its values are the medium itself. Its cultural and intellectual experiences are more and more saturated with the media and messages of modern cultures. The result is an even more radical assimilation of modern ways of life and values.[7] The renewed crisis, which all religions and cultures originating in earlier cultural mediums are now undergoing (e.g., Catholic renewal, "death of God," Black Christianity, etc.) due to the fact that the ground of society is now saturated with the new medium, is matched in the Jewish community by an even greater propensity for dissolution in the universal culture. The Jewish community (as all communities in America—only more so) is now open to positive assimilation (in both biological and cultural senses) as it has never been.[8] Even its Jewishly committed components are more influenced by the general culture than ever before —*vide* the emergence of psychedelic and radical movements among the religiously educated and committed as well as among the marginal Jews.[9] Thus the question of its survival becomes more of a question. The openness and permeability of the universal culture also cruelly test and underscore the weakness of the initial adjustment to modernization made by most Jewish institutions of value and identity transmission —i.e., the synagogues and schools, Jewish recreational institutions, and communal activities and life. Many of these adjustments worked as long as the medium was semipermeable because both cultural shelter and exclusion operated to stabilize Jewish ethnicity and values. The new equilibrium is leaving many institutions unable to function well in the new circumstance, especially in values and identity transmission to the new generation which is adapted and culturally and intellectually evolved to the new medium.

The focal point of this shift of the ground of being, as I have argued elsewhere, is the university setting.[10] Here the new universal culture is at its peak of influence, saturation and reality correspondence. The explosive factor is, of course, that eighty percent plus (going on maximum possible) of eligible Jewish students go to the university. This fact brings the rank and file of the future Jewish community (and not just an elite tempered by a lagging mass) into the new cultural medium. The negative effects of this setting on Jewish identity and loyalty (although not to some of its better values which are now enshrined in the universal culture) make inevitable that that part of the Jewish community which seeks continuity and future will turn its attention to the campus as a medium of Jewish life and future. Indeed, some, if not most, of the exceptional growth of chairs of Jewish Studies on the secular campus in the past ten years has been financed by members of the Jewish community.[11] Sometimes directly and sometimes indirectly such sponsors have recognized that, in some way, they hoped to make a positive Jewish presence and content, models and links to some aspect of Jewishness, available on campus where the students are. Projecting present trends and concern, and deducting for the gap between rhetoric and action, it is fair to predict that there will be more rather than less of such support in the future. Most of this support will grow from the Jewish community's hope and desire to assure Jewish continuity, to hold or win the respect of its young by being present on the college campus in intellectually respectable and socially accepted ways. It is unlikely that such supporters will remain indifferent to the actual effects of such study programs on Jewish commitment.

The second factor which is likely to make Judaic scholarship and teaching the focus of Jewish identity and continuity concerns is the changing nature of the Jewish student. Side by side with the majority of Jewish students' greater involvement in the universal culture and consequent distance from the particularist Jewish community, is an emerging minority "new breed" of more Jewishly committed students.[12] Many of them stock the courses that Judaica scholars are giving. Although no survey has been made of Judaica students' motives and attitudes, personal experience, (unscientific) impressions, and reports of others indicate that the bulk of students in Judaica courses are not professional journeymen preparing for careers, or even humanists studying another culture. They tend to be Jewish students expressing their positive identification by studying Jewish Studies or searchers interested in new contact with Jewish civilization. There is also another newly emerging phenomenon: the student who actively works for a greater Jewish presence on or about campus and seeks Jewish Studies as the expression of this drive. One might cite the Hebrew House established at Oberlin, or the off-campus Jewish Studies at Berkeley set up in reaction to the black studies thrust and the rejection by black militants of integrated white Jewish participation in the civil-rights struggle. Another striking example of this trend is the student and young faculty organized petitions for the initiation of modern Jewish studies at Cornell after the black studies and black enclave living furor at that school. This campaign for Jewish Studies came on a campus, where, in the past, students who opted for a "ghettoized" Jewish community living (the Young Israel house) were viewed as marginal and irrelevant by the general Jewish student population. To achieve their demands, the students pressed for the entire gamut of popular agitation, i.e., teach-ins, demonstrations, etc., and were antagonistic to the senior Jewish faculty for playing an "Uncle Jake" (Jewish "Uncle Tom") role in this matter. Add to this: the collapse of most pre-college Jewish Studies backgrounds (such as Talmud Torah and Sunday-school education) within a few weeks of exposure to the current level of scholarly understanding of religion and culture, in general, and Judaism, in particular; the absence of even such limited backgrounds for many students; the likelihood of further pressures for ethnic studies and socially generated ethnic awareness. All this suggests that the needs and demands of at least a minority of Jewish students for Jewish Studies, not only as academic discipline but as agent of self-discovery and even psychic liberation, seem likely to grow.

The third new factor for increased Jewish concern on more and more campuses is the Judaica scholar. He, I fear, will bear the burden of the new emerging claims. And to him the bulk of my analysis of options will be directed.

The Judaica scholar is, of course, a professional making his livelihood in the academic world. As such, he undergoes the professional training, tends to adopt the professional values, and to live within the campus community, such as it exists.[13] Hence, he tends to internalize the canons of objectivity, the value-free nonteleological research and methodology which, until recently, have been the consensus of the campus. An important part of him and his professional conscience tell him that there is nothing different about his scholarship and results that reflects covert assumptions and value goals, and that he has not knowingly distorted his conclusions because he is dealing with Jewish material. True, the growing sophistication of cultural analysis may make him aware of the inescapability of some *Zeitgeist,* cultural and personal subjectivity, etc.[14] He may even—after viewing the patterned divergence of modern Biblical scholarship schools, for example—ask whether there is not, after all, a Jewish point of view.[15] But he would be likely to see such divergences as perspective curvatures to be allowed for, rather than norms to be embraced or expanded. Moreover, insofar as he lives in a campus community, he is thereby brought into a social milieu with certain highly characteristic tendencies. Milton Gordon has suggested that the intellectuals—particularly in a campus community—constitute an emergent fourth ethnic subculture of American society paralleling the tri-pot, Protestant-Catholic-Jewish pattern.[16] Nor is there any secret as to the kind of religious consensus—despite the growing variety of faculty and colleges and the pressure of new ethnic movements in American life— which still tends to be most characteristic of this community. In the words of Rabbi Henry Cohen, it is "a naturalism whose faith is in the rational order of efficient causation; whose method is science, whose morality is humanism and whose messianic hope is the redemption of mankind through man's self-understanding and rationality."[17] In short, it is a consensus which is universalistic in a non-pluralist sense, and which tends to rate low certain cultural characteristics which have been prominent in Jewish culture and religion historically. Notwithstanding radical and ethnic challenges, one may guess that this consensus still dominates. Here we may face the first difference between general faculty people and our hypothesized Judaica scholar. Although no one has made a qualified survey of the Judaica scholar, personal observation suggests he is statistically less likely to be completely in this community. Likely as not, he is differentially located in a more particularist Jewish social setting; and he is someone whose career has grown out of strong Jewish roots and education, someone with concern for Jewish ethnic and/or value continuity. Moreover, to be candid, until recently his location in the university curriculum for the most part has tended to give a partial shelter or particularist flavor to his habitat. Such a background predisposes him to involvement with Jewish survival.

There is a strong professional factor which tends to block Judaic scholars' involvement in Jewish value concerns. By and large, the key to academic success and advancement remains research pursued and published in accordance with the dominant norms of the academic community. Thus, in a real sense, every act of student involvement, Jewish community concern or value activity is potentially or actually in competition for the precious time, energy, and immersion needed for professional growth. Since Jewish Studies have only recently and, to some extent, only partially (especially in a geographical sense) attained academic respectability, there is an additional pressure against too close an identification with the concerns of the Jewish community and for the Jewish civilization. Nor is the campus community as pluralist toward particularist Jewish concerns as it seems to be becoming toward other ethnic concerns. (Apparently societal, personal and financial pressures, if strongly enough applied, are not without effect despite their non-legitimacy by the official standards of the academic community.) Yet, as a concerned member of the Jewish community, one subject to its social and intellectual pulls, as a Jew who may care about Jewish continuity, the Judaica scholar may find both inner and external pressures for various forms of involvement. Undoubtedly individuals will respond differently depending on their own hierarchy of values and concerns and on different temperaments, influences, etc. An important factor will be the relative psychic independence of the individual vis-à-vis the campus and general American culture. Here I suspect a generation gap may unfold. Or perhaps a combination generation and atmosphere of education gap may unfold—with younger men and men educated in more open settings (psychologically if not academically) more likely to diverge from the general campus norms.

Now what possible responses can the Judaica teacher then give to the tacit or overt call for help from the Jewish student and community, for more help with Jewish identity and continuity?

One possible option is to draw firmer the professional line and to shut out these claims. There is a trend to greater integration of Jewish Studies in the general curriculum as well as in such organizations as the American Academy of Religion (which themselves are moving more into the mainstream). The Judaica scholar might indeed follow Gerson Cohen's prescription and simultaneously encourage the Jewish community to further support the establishment of Judaica chairs while rejecting any attempt to use the chairs as "stimuli and aids to Jewish identity and pride on the campus."[18] Since it is obvious that the prime motive of community giving would be the promise or hope of the denied function, one could question the moral adequacy of such a line and point to the gap between the hopes raised (even if non-verbally) and the overt denial of responsibility. Of course, it can be argued that "the mere presence of Jewish Studies on the campus, provided they are a fair representation of the totality of Jewish life and are treated as an academic discipline, are by their presence an affirmation of the corporate identity of the Jews."[19] It is true that the respectability factor alone, the recognition of the equality of Judaism as a scholarly humanities endeavor serves as one of the few positive models of Jewishness as present and equal on campus. This factor of respectability is characteristically over-rated by the older generation which is still hung up on and impressed by the achievement of acceptance in American cultural settings. It tends to impress the younger generation considerably less. Youth takes its at-homeness for granted and tends to measure teachers simply by their performance in the general cultural competition. Paradoxically, then, the greater assimilation of the younger generation makes it less impressed by the mere fact of Jewish acceptance yet more open to Jewish—or non-Jewish—influence. Nevertheless, Judaic scholarship is one kind of model needed for a positive Jewish identity on campus. Thus, Judaica academics can insist on following natural academic and research bents ignoring Jewish considerations, arguing that their free enterprise efforts, by a kind of natural guiding hand, would serve the best particularist interests of the Jewish community. They might even indignantly add that it is now clearly recognized by American society and capitalism that, although they pay the bills, the university can and should serve as critic, not merely propagandist, of the system which feeds it. Shall Jewish Studies then be confirmed as "inferior" by accepti.g the rights of the piper payer to make greater demands upon those in this field?

One objection to this response is the now recognized objection to the Adam Smith economic version thereof: it fits too well the maximal economic and social needs of the privileged group it is written for. A second problem is the internal one: the identification with Jewish continuity. The suspicion will not down that a minimal contribution from such a pool of talent will help seal the doom of Jewish continuity in America. Moreover, it is too easy to set up this alternative as "the faculty man [being pressured] to serve as a quasi-chaplain or advocate of any form of affiliation, or for that matter of disaffiliation."[20] Most Judaica scholars, out of identification with current academic values or by pragmatic judgment that such a role will not work, will reject such an alternative. Similarly, almost all would reject the excessive ethnicism paralleling other overreactions which would claim that only Jews can teach Judaism. They, similarly, want to avoid the kind of putting identity needs first which would resent the introduction of ambiguity or insufficiency into needed heroic models, such as seems to have characterized the Nat Turner literary controversy. Besides, the breakdown of a monolithic tradition and/or consensus of values is a fact, and even a norm, in the humanities and in Jewish culture. Therefore, the teacher cannot serve in good conscience as a spokesman for any one version of the entire tradition or for the Jewish community as it sees itself.

The real question is: whether the value system and operating framework which scholars, individually and collectively, seek to foster in the field of Judaica shall include the claim or the expectation of time and effort set aside for the sake of Jewish continuity—beyond the effort in academic research. Or, in the same spirit: whether one might expect some effort and concern to properly orient the campus community and academic curriculum to do justice to the past and present life of Jewry. Of course, individuals will vary in how much of this they take up. But it is in the peer group's power to create a force field of expectation and judgment which can materially affect individual responses. Such efforts would undoubtedly create tensions in Judaica scholars between professional obligations and Jewish community needs; between vocational and avocational efforts; between the two community worlds they share. Nor should anyone underestimate the potential tension with the conventions and intellectual asymmetries of the campus community whose world Judaica scholars must inhabit professionally, if not after hours. The justification for such efforts can only come out of the depths of identification with Jewish continuity; out of the recognition that a generation which has lived through such events as the holocaust and the rebirth of Israel should feel itself charged with special obligations; and out of agreement that the crisis of Jewish continuity is so critical that more total involvement by Judaica scholars is needed to maximize chances of overcoming. These assumptions can hardly be "proven." To some extent, scholars can debate their validity and probably respond differentially in accordance with individual analyses. But, mostly, the pre-existence of such convictions must be assumed and acted upon. They are ontological to Jewish existence today and like all basic axioms, they are given and recognized, not deduced or justified.

The effort which would involve the least tension with current frames of reference and with the campus community would be the further extension of Jewish Studies—to campuses where it is not present, in scope and depth where it is found, and in new methods of cooperation to utilize collective resources to round out limitations of the small departments that now exist. Here I would endorse Gerson Cohen's excellent analysis of graduate and undergraduate pedagogy in Judaica and what can be done to improve it. The extension of Jewish Studies involves some need to make the campus community aware of the gross simplification, and even distortion, of the Jewish Studies picture it has created with its haphazard setups. These are typically one-man departments demanding general over-survey courses and spreading scholarly teaching resources thin. Equally and especially scandalous is the absence of Jewish Studies in schools where the Jewish student population and potential demand for such studies is so great. Here it should be pointed out that

Jewish Studies are not only legitimate as part of the humanities, but that instituting them is an extension of the attempt to break the current unselfconscious Western, Christian (even if in secularized form), white ethnocentrism of the "universal" university curriculum.[21] Nor should there be hesitation to point out the relevance of such studies to a Jewish student population. This can be done while avoiding the excesses of racism potential in such an approach. Perhaps the outstanding scandal in this area is the continuing absence of major Jewish Studies centers in the New York City public university system although its student population is probably well over eighty percent Jewish. This is at a time when the less than ten percent Negro and Puerto Rican students are legitimately and appropriately demanding the availability of ethnic studies which are of particular interest to them.

There is a narrow line to be walked here. Jewish Studies is solid enough not to have to ride current waves of community action or relevance. Moreover, the current wave of ethnic studies appears to be thinly capitalized in academic goals, scholarly personnel, and methodology. Such an approach could spell eventual disillusionment and scholarly bankruptcy—not to mention the possibility of ultimate academic backlash. There is no reason for Jewish Studies to be tied to such a potential albatross. But, admitting all this and, hopefully, avoiding such errors, expansion of Jewish Studies can become part of the legitimate thrust to create a truly ecumenical and pluralist academic curriculum.

This brings up an additional stage of involvement and tension. The present general-studies curriculum, it can be argued, does not do justice to Jewish civilization in many ways. As I have stated elsewhere: "The university, and its curriculum, is secular and nonsectarian by its own definition. Thus the student is apt to take its presentation of Judaism at face value. Judaism and Jewish History is presented in passing in many of the college curriculums—such as the ubiquitous Social Science I or Humanities I courses. However, the presentation here turns out to be essentially a secularized version of traditional Christian stereotypes of Judaism."[22] Judaism tends to disappear after the birth of Christ—perhaps to reappear with Martin Buber, more likely not to reappear. Similarly, one should point to the stereotypes which tend to underestimate the significance of Jewish particularist existence and religion which circulate freely in the conventional social medium of the campus community. Such views will tend to persist like all cultural stereotypes until (and somewhat beyond) they are challenged by scholarship, personal contact with people who know better in depth, and until alternate images are presented.[23] The average Humanities textbook and teacher will remain blissfully ignorant of Yehezkel Kaufmann unless there is a more conscious polemic and organized lobbying. Such a task would logically fall to Judaica scholars who have the requisite scholarship and concern. But they would have to be willing to risk condemnation or resistance from an official universalism which is not often ready to admit its failures in practice. The precious newly won "respectability" might be sneered at as the particularist concerns draw resentment. (Such sneering would likely stem especially from Jews seeking to escape to the universal culture.)

There is another more subtle area where Judaica scholars could make a contribution to the viability of Judaism and Jewish culture while operating within conventional academic norms. All of the particularist ethos, including Judaism, are suffering a loss of believability now that they have entered into the oikumene—for their language and transmissions were shaped in an ethnocentered world. The result was an inevitable "curvature" of language and concept to favor the home culture and a "distortion" of perspective and even content of alternate value systems and cultures. This once helped assure continuity. But in an open cultural situation, this becomes dysfunctional. As the student experiences the reality of the other culture, it destroys the believability of the inherited system. Such a factor frequently makes Jewish knowledge and values appear to be weaker in truth than they are intrinsically. Here the Judaica scholar, as he moves with the general world of knowledge and lives with the "other" systems, can play a big role in the reorientation of Jewish language and perspective needed to retain believability and to make the positive Jew an honest and truthful citizen of the new and, more and more, one world of culture.[24]

All of these examples involve the use of the professional in academic areas albeit with broadened ambit. There is, however, another way in which academic skills can enrich the Jewish community. It involves going off campus or, at least, applying academic skills to currently off-campus concerns. In the increasingly complex and technological world we live in, the universities have become major clusters of skills and expertise. These are supplied to society to enable it to function at the level it must.[25] Such trends are continually accelerating despite the current outcry at university military research. When elementary and secondary education (especially in the sciences) needed to be upgraded, the impetus and leadership was supplied by the university talent banks. Outstanding examples were the Physical Science Study Group, and the redoing of the physics-math secondary curricula led by Zacharias, and the elementary and pre-school revisions under the impact of Bruner, *et al.* Considering that elementary and secondary Jewish education is so utterly inadequate, this is probably the major area where a great contribution can be made by Judaica scholars. This could involve new curricula, textbooks, mass media, etc. The Melton Institute program gives an inkling of the potential impact of the conceptual and intellectual upgrading and sophistication of the Jewish curriculum. Of course this would take not only involvement and thinking power, but a willingness to play the role of critic of the present situation, of lobby for new spending, etc. Given the prestige of academia and the great void in the Jewish community, but discounting for the entrenched irrelevance of many organizations and professionals and the ongoing control of community spending by wealthy but ignorant and Jewishly uninterested laymen, there is still much that could be done. Without underestimating the difficulties involved, pressure from an organized body of Judaica scholars collectively assembled might be particularly influential.

A similar judgment might be made on the question of upgrading Jewish professionals such as rabbis, educators, social workers, and community executives. For the most part, their Jewish education has been received in sheltered, parochial environments—marked by special or denominational pleading, low standards of intellectual and conceptual performance, etc. Bringing such people into an academic setting which is meeting the performance standards expected by society at large and unsheltered by the sentimental and nostalgic allowances for Jewish heart as opposed to substance, could do more than increase their knowledge. It could lift their performances to new levels of conceptual grasp and sophistication—multiplying the force of their efforts many fold. If a direct academic setting may be out of reach of such people, some hybrid form—say an institute or study-center setting run by academics and meeting academic standards—may be needed.[26] Following the pattern of upgrading Christian seminaries, Hebrew teachers, colleges of rabbinical seminaries can also be brought onto campus or closer to it. Since hundreds of millions of dollars are spent annually on synagogues, Jewish schools, etc., the effect of such an upgrading in terms of yield in Jewish relevance and viability could be enormous.

Such an involvement by Judaica scholars in the Jewish community can perhaps learn from the model of academic involvement with the "military-industrial complex" to avoid certain errors. This involvement need not be purely with the Jewish establishment. It should not be—

for the sake of the Jewish community in its current state of life and values. Academics should appeal from the living Jewish status quo to the living Jewish tradition which they have experienced in their own research and teaching. With all the faults, conflicting values, and primitivisms Jewish civilization has in its past, surely at its best (however defined) it is more than the over-Americanized, superficially modern, excessively hung up middle-class complex that is so much of Jewish community and life in America. Here one can draw upon the naturally critical, even alienated, tone which Judaica scholars may derive from the academic culture and medium in which they live. These tendencies can be channeled to a vitally needed critique of the current Jewish community situation. This is not to urge the assumption of the intrinsic superiority of campus community mores over anything in the Jewish community. Behind its façade of plutocracy, easy sentimentality, and tribalism, there are components of responsibility and decency in the Jewish community which the academic community has not always matched. The more creative possibility is the Judaica scholar as a dialectical moralist, able to infuse a needed note of criticism, universalism, moral fervor and/or sophistication into the Jewish community, while utilizing the organic culture and sense of continuity and human responsibility of the Jewish community and tradition as lasts to which the campus community should be fit.

Finally, there is one more most difficult and complex aspect of the Judaica scholar's relationships to Jewish continuity, beyond his career considerations: his relationship to Jewishly interested Jewish students and to Jewish members of the campus community. By and large the Jewish faculty members and students are the most alienated from Jewish culture and tradition.[27] (Even where they may be revolting for the sake of classic Jewish values such as social justice or peace, they tend to see these values as universal and as involving repudiation of Jewish particularity.) Even the positive and committed Jewish students (except for a minority which seeks a ghetto in Jewish Studies) tend to be more alienated from the Jewish models offered by the community such as rabbis, teachers, etc. For most people a link to any tradition can come only through a person himself steeped in and committed to the tradition. There can be no one tradition offered—the diversity of values and backgrounds of the Judaica scholars guarantees this. But surely the Judaica scholars are obvious foci for people seeking positive models to relate to. Since the Jewish brain drain is particularly intense in the university, the establishment of relationship with positive Jews as such could be a major force in reducing this loss of the flower of Jewish intelligence and concern.

Such a possibility, with its implied demands on time and energy, is somewhat threatening. It undoubtedly offends those who went into Jewish Studies fully determined to be detached, scholarly and not pastoral —a character type which differentially is attracted to academic life. Some scholars instinctively recoil from or actively reject such a role. This reaction may even be necessary for survival as private persons and as scholars. On the other hand, if Jewish students continue to be affected by general campus currents, they may seek out and aggressively force such an involvement. (The suggestions on using academic talents to upgrade rabbis, educators, etc., above, may thus appear as an attempt to provide alternate people to play this role—a kind of "heading off the Indians at the pass" attempt.) When all is said and done some of this role may yet fall to the lot of Jewish Studies professors. Their response can range from serving as a model and guide to Jewish knowledge and learning, or from serving as a model of self-respecting rootedness in Jewish values and community, to exemplar of Jewish concern for Jewish or societal problems. They may simply serve as a paradigm of personal ways of living Jewishly. Taking this role up positively would add significantly to the survival resources of the Jewish community. Such a contribution might truly be appreciated by a Zunz redivivus even if he might be surprised at the unexpected liveliness of the culture he sought to record and "preserve."

It would be hard to overestimate the tensions involved in trying to play such a role. It involves time and effort which is neither recognized nor rewarded by the standards of the profession as they are now defined. Perhaps the Jewish Studies departments can create some internal mechanisms of recognition, at least for teaching and time spent with students. This solution runs into the problem or possibility of further integration of Jewish Studies into more general departments. This tendency, which is preferable for raising standards further and for increasing the communication of particularist models, would presumably make special recognition criteria impossible. Perhaps there is some dialectical solution again here—that Jewish Studies be simultaneously incorporated into the general departments they fit, and yet function as an interdisciplinary meeting group as well. One suspects that only breakthroughs and widening of the concepts of the general academic community will provide a framework broad enough to meet the needs described. One is tempted also to propose that the Jewish community finance time off for the Judaica scholar to devote to its concern. The danger there is that he should primarily function on campus where he is most needed, most in tune with the medium, and most influential. The ultimate answer to this role can only be clarified by further developments in campus life and further growth in numbers and Jewish concern of Judaica scholars.

All that is described in this article is far beyond the capacity of single scholars. Perhaps it exceeds the capacity of the collective Jewish scholars. If we add to these concerns, the enormous academic and scholarly efforts and upgrading of the Judaica field needed, it seems crystal clear that there must be some community and professional organization for Judaica scholars on campus. Community may be more important than professional organization. The concerns for identity, transmission, and survival are not easily organizable or to be expressed in formal administration. The intangibles of peer groups, social mores, self-identity, shared culture, play a far greater role in determining individual responses than anything else. There is a need to turn to the model of fellowship and scholarship set by the Pharisees when Jews and Judaism faced a great cultural crisis in the first centuries. Insofar as Judaic scholars hear the call of continuity and of the future, they cannot avoid considering such models. The limits of person and the structures of today may preclude this generation from making the decisive contribution which the Pharisees made. But to quote one of them: "It is not your obligation to finish the work—but you are not at liberty to desist from [starting] it."

NOTES

1. *Etwas über die rabbinische Literatur* in L. Zunz, *Gesammelte Schriften*, I, pp. 1–31.

2. Gerson D. Cohen, "The Embarrassment of Riches: Reflections on American Jewish Scholarship in 1969"; in this volume, p. 135.

3. Michael Meyer, *The Origins of the Modern Jew*, Wayne State U. Press, (Detroit: 1967), p. 161.

4. Quoted, *ibid*, p. 161. The reader is referred for Zunz's goals to the fine chapter on Zunz in Meyer's book.

5. Gershom Scholem, "Mitoch Hirhurim Al Chochmat Yisroel" (Reflections on Jewish Scholarship) in *Luach Ha-Aretz li-shnat Tasah* (Israel Year Book 1944) (Tel Aviv: 1944) pp. 94–112.

6. The terms are Zunz's in *On Rabbinic Literature*.

7. On the achievement of modernization see my comments in "Adventure in Freedom—or Escape from Freedom: Jewish Identity in America," *American Jewish Historical Quarterly*, Vol. LV, No. 1 (Sept. 1965) pp. 5ff. On values change, see my earlier comments in "Jewish Values and the Changing American Ethic," *Tradition*, vol. 10, no. 1 (Summer 1968) pp. 42–74. *See also* n. 9, below.

8. The evidence for this is ubiquitous. For one recent comment on accelerating intermarriage rates, see Marshall Sklare, "Intermarriage and Jewish Survival," *Commentary* (March 1970) pp. 51–58.

9. While we lack studies of these developments, one can peruse with profit the pages of *Response Magazine, Genesis II, The Other Stand*, or see Harold Goldberg's ms. study of the "Jews for Urban Justice."

10. Irving Greenberg, "Jewish Survival and the College Campus," *Judaism*, vol. 17, no. 3 (Summer 1968), pp. 259–281.

11. On the growth of chairs of Jewish Studies, see Arnold J. Band, "Jewish Studies in American Liberal Arts Colleges and Universities," *American Jewish Year Book*, vol. 68 (1967), pp. 3–30.

12. Cf. n. 8.

13. See Christopher Jencks, "The Academic Subculture," in Roger Hagan, ed., *Character and Social Structure in America* (Cambridge, Mass.: 1960), Harvard Printing Office, offset print, pp. 95–122; and Morris Rosenberg, "Occupations and Values" in Morris Rosenberg and Paul Lazarsfeld, eds., *The Language of Social Research* (Glencoe, Ill.: 1955). *See also*, Christopher Jencks and David Reisman *The Academic Revolution*, (Garden City: 1968). *See also* n. 16 below.

14. For a recent devastating critique of these assumptions, see Alvin W. Gouldner, *The Coming Crisis of Western Sociology* Basic Books (New York: 1970).

15. Cf. Nahum Sarna's article in this book, p. 35.

16. Milton Gordon, *Assimilation in American Life*, (New York: 1964) pp. 224–232.

17. Quoted in Marshall Sklare, "Intermarriage and the Jewish Future," *Commentary*, vol. 37, no. 4, (April 1964) p. 50.

18. Gerson Cohen, *op cit,* p. 135.

19. *Ibid.*

20. *Ibid.*

21. See Emil Fackenheim's Address to the Faculty of Arts and Sciences, University of Toronto. March 30, 1970.

22. I. Greenberg, "Jewish Survival and the College Campus," *loc cit.,* p. 267.

23. See Walter Kaufmann, *Critique of Religion and Philosophy,* (Garden City: 1961). On the transmission and persistence of images, see Kenneth Boulding, *The Image,* (Ann Arbor: 1961).

24. For some comments on the reorientation of language and the effects of cultural "curvature" on believability, see I. Greenberg, "The Cultural Revolution and Religious Unity," *Religious Education* (March-April 1967), pp. 98–103.

25. Clark Kerr, *The Uses of the University* (New York: 1968). James A. Perkins, *The University in Transition* (New York: 1966) see also Jacques Barzun's critique, *The American University* (New York: 1969).

26. Cf. the proposal for a Center for Jewish Survival in "Jewish Survival," *op cit.* pp. 276–281; and I. Greenberg, "The Center for Jewish Thought and Values: A Prospectus," circulating in ms. form.

27. For some skepticism and questions on this point and some projected research in the field, see Norman L. Friedman, "The Problem of the 'Runaway Jewish Intellectuals': Social Definition and Sociological Perspective," *Jewish Social Studies,* vol. 31, no. 1, pp. 3–19.

AN EMBARRASSMENT OF RICHES:
ON THE CONDITION OF AMERICAN JEWISH
SCHOLARSHIP IN 1969

GERSON D. COHEN
Columbia University
Professor of History

OVER one hundred and fifty years have passed since Leopold Zunz first issued his impassioned plea for intensive and dispassionate study of the whole corpus of post-Biblical Jewish literature, and for the incorporation of this so-called "Rabbinic literature" in the agenda of scientific investigation of the past. Were Zunz alive today, judging solely on the basis of his explicit statements in the epoch-making essay, *Etwas ueber die Rabbinische Litteratur,* he would probably be ecstatic with joy. Virtually every one of the areas which he enumerated as requiring intensive research, and several new ones of which he could not possibly even have dreamed, have become the objects of tireless study and of scholarly treatment in many countries. What is more, world scholarly opinion has by and large renounced, at least publicly, the studied neglect of Jewish history and culture that stares one in the face on virtually every page of Gentile scholarship on the Jews and Judaism until the latter part of the nineteenth century and, indeed, in many scholarly tracts down to the Second World War. Zunz could never have guessed that Jewish books would be far more available in 1969 than they were in 1919, a year which he explicitly mentioned as one that would be too late for any fundamental research in Judaica! Would Zunz, Steinschneider, or even Graetz have believed that in 1969 some fifty professors of Judaica, to a considerable degree American-born and trained, representing but a moiety of the universities sponsoring programs in Jewish studies and reflecting but a portion of the fields studied and taught, would gather at a major American university established by Jews to consider the status of their profession? Our presence at the conference is one among many, but by no means the most trivial of testimonies belying Zunz's pessimistic prognosis of 1818.

We could go on in this vein endlessly. Each one of us here, and many

135

many more who are not, could add his—or, let it not be overlooked, *her* —personal footnote in testimony to Jewish scholarly achievements and attainments beyond the most daring dreams of the fathers of *juedische Wissenschaft*. The seeds sown by these pioneers have yielded great fruits, many of which it has been the privilege of our generation to reap. We have witnessed a period in which the Jews with their culture, their scholarship and their overall physical dignity and security have emerged from the worst catastrophe in their history proud and productive, strengthened and determined. Never before have Jews played so active a role in the affairs of the world in general, and in the academic world in particular, as equals and as of right. We have become a part of the mainstream of Western civilization and have gained recognition for our identity—for our right to retain our past and to cultivate our future.

To keep our eyes fixed on the central theme of our own particular interest, in the world of higher education and scholarship our subject matter has gained and continues to gain an ever growing foothold within that vast industrial enterprise known as Academia. In the colleges and universities of the United States and Canada, Judaic studies have finally attained the recognition and the acceptance of which the fathers of *juedische Wissenschaft* dreamed and for which their communal representatives begged in vain. The marketplace of higher learning provides a much more receptive and encouraging face today than it did a quarter of a century ago to competent, or even to merely aspiring, talents in every area of Jewish research. There are no longer twenty able, eager and available Jewish scholars for every post. How long this burgeoning trend will continue I will not venture to guess. For the present, the market for Judaica is inviting and has become sufficiently large and populous to generate several studies and surveys and this initiatory convocation.

Underneath the surface of these salutary phenomena there lurk some disquieting aspects that disturb even the Pollyannas of our group. We are confronted by a kind of conquest which gives no sure promise of continuity. Judging from present indications we may, within a relatively short span of time, come to the point where we will not have an adequate supply of qualified manpower to fill the posts available and, what is far worse, to continue Jewish research on the high level that it has attained. Indeed, the abundance of available posts has already become somewhat of an embarrassment to those of us who are consulted for advice in staffing positions in several areas of Judaica. Even recent graduates are no longer overwhelmed by every opportunity that happens their way to teach the subject matter of their own specialties. And when it comes to recommending names for premium chairs, the number of qualified and attractive candidates who would consider moving from their present positions to new ones is often a very meager one.

Accordingly, I believe the time is ripe for us to evaluate our situation, to assess the needs of our profession and to give careful consideration to specific steps that we ought to take *collectively* in keeping with the trust inherent in our posts. Only by continued pooling of our thinking and by concerted adoption of appropriate courses of action can we hope to meet the totally unprecedented challenges with which our present situation confronts us.

Professionally we have waxed and multiplied, spanned the length and breadth of our continent, and have begun to reach out and establish new footholds in others. But we have grown like Topsy, with no rhyme or reason, and frequently in response to needs and considerations far different from those we would be likely to spell out as justifying our chairs. Put bluntly, "Jewish studies" have become a catch-all that covers the whole spectrum of Jewish experience from Terah to Ben Gurion and from Megiddo to Williamsburg. The mere fact that Jewish studies appear on the roster of offerings of a college or university in no way provides even a hint of the subject matter that will be taught, let alone of the level on which the materials will be treated.

The program which the professor of Judaica teaches may in reality be one in modern Hebrew language and literature, with no reference to anybody before Mapu or Mendele, or it may be a religion program in which the Bible and the early post-Biblical period are the burden of emphasis. But whatever the content of the particular set of offerings, Jewish studies are most frequently sponsored by any one of a number of academic departments—Near Eastern Studies, Classics, Philosophy, Religion, Linguistics, History—where these studies occupy but a small share in the work and concerns of the department generally and in which, accordingly, the majority of the staff have little professional knowledge or interest. On occasion, Jewish studies are sponsored simultaneously by several different departments within one university without any coordination and interdepartmental planning on the overall program of Judaica on the campus. Frequently, the student is left to his own devices to select from this academic cafeteria those courses which appear to be most appetizing to him but which, when examined in relation to one another, provide no balanced fare and certainly no reasoned structure. From the point of view of Jewish studies as a whole, our university programs today provide largely knickknacks that are, to be sure, deeply enriching to many but hardly well planned and coherent systems that will provide students with a solid introduction to Jewish studies or intensive training in most of its subdivisions. By and large, Judaic studies today are either tailored for the most advanced students or for the most elementary and ephemeral dabblers.

There are, of course, good historical reasons for this fragmentation and imbalance, and we would be guilty of ingratitude to the pioneers in this endeavor, to whom we owe so much, were we to overlook these factors. The most urgent need felt by those working to get Judaica placed on the American campus was simply to get on the books, to achieve official recognition and sponsorship and to have Jewish scholarship represented by outstanding scholars. At the same time they were eager for Jewish studies to be incorporated in the mainstream of university activity and to avoid for their discipline the isolation and stigma of parochialism that would be imposed on their work if it should be constituted as a separate Jewish unit or—in the days when Departments of Religion were not the most intellectually scintillating and respectable corners on the campus— attached to the Department of Religion. The initiators of Judaic studies quite logically and properly strove to overcome first obstacles first. Provision of a structured program that would guide students from the rudiments through the Ph.D. level was, to those involved in those early efforts, a pipe dream or, in any case, a remote goal with which they could not be expected to concern themselves. Technical training in the linguistic and textual studies, they felt, would have to be secured in Jewish schools, *yeshivot* or seminaries, whose alumni constituted the overwhelming bulk of graduate students in Judaica until well after the Second World War.

Very suddenly, however, in the wake of the general metamorphosis that overtook American universities after 1946, college and university offerings in Judaica began almost to mushroom. Nevertheless, many of the old patterns and scholarly prejudices continued. Programs were instituted to suit the tastes of local departments, Jewish communities, and the scholars appointed to the newly created posts. Almost all of these programs paid increasing attention to students without broad backgrounds in Judaica. However, virtually none could direct its energies to the needs of the *field* as a whole or, for that matter, of any single segment within it, and to the possibility of training advanced students in Judaica exclusively within the context of the American university system.

The results are fairly obvious. Viewed from any perspective, apart perhaps from that of the scholarly research of the professors themselves, the results have been by and large haphazard, occasionally brilliant and deeply rewarding to student, teacher, and general community, most often superficial and ephemeral with no discernible effect on the student body or on the general depth of Judaica training on all levels.

Obviously we must employ different criteria for evaluation of goals and achievements in graduate and undergraduate studies. However, it is precisely after looking at university programs from these two persepctives that it seems to me that our work often falls short. In graduate studies of Judaica, which historically were the first to make their way onto the American campus, we are still largely dependent on outside agencies for the training of students in the basic skills indispensable to research in our field. In other words, we have made no substantive progress toward the creation of university programs that will enable us to reproduce ourselves professionally and provide for the continuity of natively trained scholars of high caliber. On the undergraduate level, it seems to me, we neither have reared, nor give any prospect of rearing, a college-trained lay public with any real appreciation of Jewish history, literature, and thought. Moreover, our undergraduate programs generally do not provide the propaedeutic skills to which I have just alluded and thus serve as no real introduction to graduate study and research.

My aim in these sweeping characterizations is not to indict, but to provide some tentative suggestions on the underlying causes for these situations and for some possible corrective steps that we might think of taking individually and, above all, collectively. I begin deliberately with a discussion of advanced studies for, while that area poses far more formidable technical hurdles to surmount, they are to my mind largely practical ones that are more easily disposed of in discussion than the broader area of undergraduate and overall university programs. What is more, in the final analysis we will be judged as scholars and teachers individually and collectively, by the extent to which we have contributed to knowledge. I do not believe that I need argue that this contribution must be not only scholarly publication but also—and what to my mind is of at least equal importance—the raising of a new generation that will be capable of carrying on our work and expanding its horizons. Hence, graduate study is our seedbed for future scholarship.

Up to this point students of Judaica have had to come with Talmud in hand, and they have, accordingly, come almost exclusively from rabbinical seminaries or their surrogates, or from Israel and its educational network. That was to be expected, and I do not believe that these sources will, or should, ever be totally displaced. Some of our students will continue to come from, or repair for further training to Israel and Jewish colleges and seminaries where the textual disciplines in the classical literature of the Jews are taught intensively by experts. However, until we devise the means for the training of at least some of our students in classical Jewish disciplines within the context of the university we will not be able to claim to have come of age.

I am not in any way urging or even hoping that every graduate department of Judaica should provide the facilities for propaedeutic, let alone advanced, training in all the fields of classical Judaica. Clearly no American university is likely to have the means at its disposal to undertake such a program in the foreseeable future. Nevertheless, I do believe that we could devise facilities for making these techniques available to the students in the field. There is no reason why we could not pool our scattered and fragmented resources and create, for classical Judaica, the kind of consortium for intensive technical training that other esoteric and inaccessible disciplines have formed in the United States. By offering joint programs on different campuses on a rotating basis we would all benefit, without placing impossible obstacles before our universities and students alike. What is required is organization of the resources at our disposal and administrative responsibility to the field as a whole rather than to any single institution.

A far knottier challenge, and one that faces us with ever growing proportions, is the overall image of Jewish studies on the university campus. More and more of us are being called upon to devote ever increasing proportions of our energies to undergraduate teaching, or to the introduction of students on all university levels to Jewish history, literature and thought. Here again we confront fragmentation, imbalance and, above all, disproportionate emphasis on certain aspects of Jewish history and experience at the expense of others that are at least as vital to a proper understanding of Jewish culture. Frequently tailoring our instruction in accordance with values which we have inherited from German Jewish *Wissenschaft* or the East European Enlightenment

Revival, we all too often neglect those very areas that constitute the major portion of classical Jewish history, thought, and literature. I have reference to the span of Jewish history from Ezra to the Emancipation, to Rabbinic literature (in the wider sense that Zunz used the term) including pre-modern secular Jewish literature, and to corporate Jewish life, especially in the diaspora, from the Amoraic period until the emergence of the State of Israel. Equally worrisome is the lack of any consensus, tacit or articulated, on what constitutes the minimum content and extent of the material that should be transmitted by any given college or university cycle. As a consequence, even the student who has taken a full roster of offerings in Judaica, indeed even a major in Hebrew language and literature, can, and frequently does, emerge from his college and university experience with a very spotty—superficial goes without saying, but spotty is the crux word here—sampling of Jewish culture. The student is likely to have had at least one course in Bible—including a survey course on "the Old Testament," but not necessarily a survey, of post-Biblical Hebrew literature. And if a survey course in post-Biblical Hebrew literature is provided, the real nature and content of Amoraic activity, of Gaonic literature, of the medieval codes, commentaries, poetic corpora, philosophic treatises, and pietistic tracts are more often than not totally omitted. We may assert the contrary all we like, but in our official acts we often echo the prejudices of Gentile and some Jewish secularist savants that the mantle of Jewish vitality and creativity passed from the Psalmist to Mendele, from Bar Kokhba to Herzl, from the Pharisees to Buber.

What I am bemoaning for the moment is not the general survey courses, when and where they are provided, but the lack of them and, more important, the lack of agreement as to what they should cover.

To some extent, it is true, the gaps in the basic training of our undergraduate programs are a consequence of the administrative fragmentation of Jewish studies under various departments, the very names of which either purport to absolve us of responsibility or perhaps inhibit our coverage of material that we know to be essential to a basic and well-rounded program. Is it the province of the Hebrew language and literature man to teach about Jewish settlements in the Middle Ages or about Jewish religious development? Those clearly are the responsibilities of the Jewish history professor and of the instructor of religious studies. Obviously. But alas, how many universities in the country provide courses in Judaica in three different departments, or for that matter within one department, so that the undergraduate may have available to him the kind of balanced and diversified program that is available to the student of classics, of English history and literature, of Chinese and Japanese civilizations? The time has come for us to make explicit to the academic world at large that Jewish studies cover a huge variety of fields, and that if we are to have any hope, not only of recruiting prospective and knowledgeable scholars in the field, but of having Jewish culture appreciated and understood humanistically, students must have available to them more than disjointed samplers of Jewish history and culture.

Such a program and reorientation of administrators of college curricula, I am fully aware, are somewhat utopian at present and not likely to be implemented within a short period. All kinds of considerations, some of them quite legitimate from the point of view of men who must apportion never too plentiful funds in accordance with the needs and consensus of their major constituencies, are likely to stop us dead in our tracks for the foreseeable future. After all, one of the very few real departments of Jewish studies in this country, in a secular university established and run principally by Jews, felt compelled to attach its program to Near Eastern studies. And if the one secular Jewish university in this country did not feel free to dedicate a department exclusively to Jewish studies, what should we expect of state and private universities with relatively smaller demands for Jewish programs? For the present, therefore, we shall have to make do with what we have and try to act as best we can upon the needs we recognize.

Granted that the facilities at our disposal are by and large quite inadequate to provide a fully balanced program of studies in Judaica, I think it would be wrong not to make at least some mention of a quite different consideration operating within our own minds. Scholarly canons and professional inhibitions, I believe, often actually militate in our circle against doing anything to rectify the situation. Given the extent and kaleidoscopic picture of Jewish studies, it is reasoned, any survey of Jewish history and literature must inevitably be thin, superficial, dilettantish. We have become, it seems, so wary of being uncritical *maskilim* and of creating a new generation of them, that we tend to forget that *maskilim* were Jewish humanists, and the least a student of Judaica should get is a basic introduction and orientation to the Jewish humanities, to Jewish civilization in all its major facets and developments. A general grounding in Judaica should mean, at the very least, a basic familiarity with the history of Jewish settlement and migration, the development of Jewish thought, literature, and institutions, and finally the fundamental motifs and processes recurring in, and affecting the course of Jewish history and culture. In short, the student must have acquired a new and sophisticated appreciation of such basic terms as the Jews, Judaism, Jewish history. We cannot afford to leave elementary training and basic orientation for graduate studies. If our long-range professional goals have always been quite clear—and they are, I suppose, to pursue, cultivate, and disseminate scholarly research by our own work and through the training of competent graduates—our immediate techniques and standards for various levels of qualifying have by no means been so apparent. My own experience with many students has convinced me that standards and programs for meeting them are quite disparate and arbitrary. Confronted with a student who has taken Judaica courses in college over a period of years one has no guarantee of what pivotal and fundamental areas of Jewish history and culture the student has in any way even tasted.

Many of us, and I include myself, have long bemoaned the fact that this situation is equally true of students who have spent years in primary and secondary Jewish day schools. *Yeshiva* education has been abysmally one-sided, uncritical, unchallenging, and almost totally unrelated to the wider intellectual world which the student will have to face in college or shortly thereafter. All of us have encountered graduates of these programs who can recite whole chunks from Isaiah, the Mishnah, and the Babylonian Talmud without having the foggiest notion of Jewish history, of Jewish religious development, or even of the content of *piyyutim* they have been taught to recite liturgically. Indeed, not one out of a hundred of these graduates knows how to read Hebrew properly, even if the text before him is pointed with vowels and accent marks. The suggestion that the prayer book merits reading as a structured complex of ideas strikes him as bizarre and trivial. Ask him the difference between Rashi and the Meharsha, and he is likely to say that one is printed on the margin and the other in the back of Talmudic tractates. Who they were, when and where they lived, and what motivated each of them—that is a preocupation of *goyyim* who cannot "learn."

However this parochialism will be defended or explained, the fact remains that we can no longer even count on Jewish day schools to provide us with a source of properly prepared students, as our teachers could on graduates of European *yeshivot* and of Rabbinical seminaries in the United States. The *yeshivot* today have provided neither the knowledge nor the stimulus for the pursuit of advanced Jewish studies, at least critically and with an effort at objectivity. On the college level, and often enough in graduate school, we must begin training from scratch even with products of day schools.

If anything must be articulated in the very near future, it seems to me, it is a clear definition of the Jewish humanities with a set of standards which will clarify, on various levels, to be sure, and with all due attention to the different areas encompassed by Jewish studies, what we conceive to be the proper scope of Judaica, what we regard as minimal requirements for a college program of Jewish studies and what are the prerequisites for graduate study in the field. Once we have such general blueprints and standards, the various degrees of excellence in Jewish studies will become apparent to everyone of themselves.

We dare not dodge this task under the guise of academic freedom or because such definitions constrict the free soaring of inquiry. Let me hasten to emphasize that I am not requesting any written set of standards or any kind of syllabus that will serve as a code for college programs in Judaica. What I am hoping is that gatherings such as this will help to generate a community of professors of Judaica, a community and not an occupational union, a community of spirit and of vision that works within a consensus. Now, consensus need not, probably should not, be written down or codified, but it should nonetheless be articulated until it is at least roughly clear. Moreover, our consensus is likely to change as times change and as new men and women join our ranks. We owe it to them no less than to our students and ourselves to try to formulate a common and meaningful universe of discourse that is flexible and plastic enough to allow for individual variation as well as for periodic review and critical appraisal.

*   *   *

In all fairness we must emphasize that the fragmentation and consequent disorientation that have beset our field are, of course, by no means unique to Judaic studies. The lack of common objectives, programs and techniques, and the complaint over the chaotic educational and intellectual atmosphere, are symptomatic of the wider university scene of which we are but a small part. Even if we should attempt to account for the problems facing us in terms of purely Jewish historical development, we would, I suspect, find that these factors are in reality subcultural manifestations of the major intellectual upheavals that have shaken the foundations of the world generally and in particular the intellectual-educational milieu everywhere. We may, accordingly, be tempted to shrug our shoulders and absolve ourselves of any special responsibility in the present tumultuous educational atmosphere. If the cedars of Cambridge, New Haven, and Morningside Heights have been unable to cope satisfactorily with their problems, what can we little hyssops do, who collectively could hardly match in size even one branch of a single major university? Indeed, any attempt on our part to suggest remedies for problems that have baffled the intellects of some of the most astute talents in the field of education in this generation would seem to smack of megalomaniacal fantasy.

But although, to be sure, the fragmentation and disintegration that have afflicted American higher education during the last two decades are in large measure consequences of the demise of old faiths—faith in the fundamental unity of all knowledge, faith in the ultimate interconnection between the humanities and the sciences, faith in the liberalizing effect of education generally and of higher liberal education in particular—we should not fear to admit that at least some share of the responsibility must be laid at the doorstep of individual disciplines, whose representatives have not given sufficient attention to challenges posed to their own fields by changes on the social, political, and educational scene. Witnessing the breakup of the pristine bonds that held the educational fabric together in the nineteenth and the early part of the twentieth centuries, they have frequently been quite complacent about letting the very same process set in within the walls of their own departments and specialties. The consequence has been that not only is there really no common universe of discourse between classicist and physicist, historian and economist, yes, even between Bible scholar and talmudist, but that even within departments there is little common vocabulary except between men sharing the same specialty. I have no messianic summons to the men of all departments to unite and break the fetters of specialization, indeed of the new intellectual parochialism that is all about us. However, I do feel that it is not a vain task for people within a common discipline to undertake.

Over and beyond all of the real and quite disturbing academic realities that I mentioned earlier as contributing to the disintegration of Judaic studies in this country, there is a far more profound challenge to our teaching that consists in a relatively new state of mind. Many of us no longer seem to be sure what the content of Judaic studies ought to be. Since, whatever our private religious commitments, we are not instructors of Torah in the traditional sense, we are, I believe, all fairly in agreement that our job is to impart the history and tools of Jewish experience and expression in all of its diverse forms. Accordingly, we feel required to give greater weight than our *yeshiva* counterparts and forbears to modern creativity and to the quest for new forms of social organizations and artistic expression. On the university campus Agnon and Dayyan must be given equal emphasis with Akiba and Bar Kokhba, the kabbalists and hasidim with the philosophers and the codifiers, sectarian deviations with the representatives of the normative mainstream. But, in consequence, most of us are quite at a loss to find any connective thread between some of the disparate, nay, often mutually antagonistic and exclusive elements on this vast tapestry of Jewish experience. Indeed, many of us have given up the once basic and widely held notion of a normative Judaism, which at least served as a touchstone with which to separate the authentic from the spurious, the normal from the deviant. Acordingly, we have lost hold of any single tradition to which we can give our intellectual allegiance and around which we can tie and evaluate the material which we feel ought to be transmitted. In short, the term "the Jewish tradition," or even "Jewish tradition" without a definite article, has ceased to have any meaning or mandate upon most of us in our professional capacities. We have thus tacitly resigned ourselves to teaching those elements of Jewish history and expression that interest *us* as scholars rather than what we have, after careful and prolonged consideration, concluded is relevant to, and vital for, the needs of our student constituencies.

The sense of tradition that we have lost did not die by default or because of any failing of the present generation of Jewish scholars. Indeed, the quandary is as keenly felt in Israel as it is here and in other countries where free scholarly inquiry has been permitted to flourish undisturbed. Exactly twenty-five years ago Professor Gershom Scholem shook the entire community of Jewish scholars by a blistering attack on the whole history of *juedische Wissenschaft* for its spiritual superficiality, duplicity, and basically Germanic orientation. Scholem called for a new spirit, a new perspective on Jewish history and creativity that would reject lock, stock, and barrel the apologetic and pseudo-universalist aims of the leading figures of German Jewish scholarship. His colleague and close associate in spirit as well as in work, Professor Yitzhak Baer, has in somewhat different ways called repeatedly for a transvaluation of nineteenth-century Jewish scholarly canons and values. But while the clarion calls of these noble and towering scholarly figures have generated respect and a bit of discussion, they have led their disciples to no really new directions, nor enabled them to discern any new and attractive horizons that would muster the loyalties and commitments of even a significant portion of the present generation. The task, in short, is more easily requested than fulfilled, and in Israel no less than here.

The problem, in a nutshell, is identical with the one besetting the humanities generally in recent years, except that in our case the task is to define or rediscover the unifying threads within one tradition rather than the relationship between several disciplines. Not very long ago, the leading spokesmen of Jewish scholarship, Schechter, Ginzberg, Kohler, Moore, and Baeck, could defend the basic integrity of Jewish tradition by distinguishing between normative and deviant Judaism. But what the immediate targets of their attack—Harnack, Bousset, Toy, and Schuerer—could not argue cogently, at least to the satisfaction of those steeped in rabbinics, the new Jewish studies of kabbalah, and the discovery of hitherto unknown mines of information about non-normative strands within Jewish history, did achieve. We can no longer dismiss Biblical criticism and its results as higher anti-Semitism; nor can we ignore the implications of the Dead Sea Scrolls, apocalyptic literature, Jewish gnostic and magical texts, Judeo-Christianity, Karaism, Jewish philosophy from Philo to the Jewish Averroists, kabbalah, Sabbatianism, hasidism and so on and on, as ephemeral or insignificant deviations of fringe groups that had no serious impact on the Jewish mainstream. For a century and more Jewish scholars proclaimed from the rooftops that Jewish culture was not a monolith or fossil, that Jewish expression and creativity were as multifaceted and as reflective of vitality as the cultural expressions and institutions of any other group. And now that scholarship has demonstrated the point, we are perplexed to find what, if anything, holds them together; we are challenged to reformulate the overall theme of our researchers and of our instruction.

* * *

In the community at large, in recent years, there has been evident an increasing interest in placing and supporting Jewish studies on the university campus, not so much as vehicles of knowledge and research for their own sake, as of stimuli and aids to Jewish identity and pride on the campus. I do not believe there can be any objection to these motives, provided they remain confined to board rooms and do not in any way interfere with the scholarly detachment essential to our work; which is to say, provided they do not in any way pressure the faculty man to serve as a quasi-chaplain or advocate of any form of affiliation, or for that matter of disaffiliation. From our point of view, the mere presence of Jewish studies on the campus, provided they are a fair representation of the totality of Jewish life and are treated as an academic discipline, are by their presence an affirmation of the corporate identity of the Jews. But to make our positions tools of propaganda and preachment for any cause, ultimate or contingent, is so reprehensible and unthinkable that if that should ever be the price for their inclusion it would be better for them not to be part of the campus complex.

I trust that I will be forgiven for reaffirming what to us are obvious principles. However, it is likely that in the coming years, owing to misappropriation and misuse of academic facilities by other groups, we will be placed under increasing pressures to depart from them just a wee bit. We would, if we should succumb, become just a little pregnant with partisanship, a taint which all of us find revolting when we encounter it in others. We should never forget or fail to remind our friends on and off campus that for a century and more Jewish studies had to contend with the university as a vehicle of Christian identity and with general refusal to allow Jewish studies to be cultivated precisely because they would become mere vessels of propaganda. Identity, in the sense that it has come to be invoked as a shibboleth by community leaders and organizations, is a genuine concern in its own place. To the extent that our work helps clarify and crystallize loyalties to the community and thus yields some social fruit, well and good. But that is a side product that must be sown and attended to elsewhere and by other agencies. If they fail, it is decidedly not our task to attempt to heal breaches they have not succeeded in managing.

On the other hand, there still remains a huge job of community education to be done with respect to the needs of our field. Quite manifestly the bulk of support for Jewish studies will have to continue to come from the same sources that it has come from in the past, namely the American Jewish community. While there have been admirable instances of endowment of chairs and even of whole programs of Judaica, the lay community has, by and large, not displayed the kind of understanding for the needs of Jewish scholarship that would permit us to look forward to the future with confidence on any level. The amount of fellowship money for the training of students, while far greater than it was twenty years ago, has been so meager as to be almost a joke. That it costs far more to train a scholar of Judaica than it does a researcher in American studies should be so obvious that it should not have to be urged. That without a native cadre of fully trained scholars, Jewish studies here will quickly decay and earn deserved contempt from any student of taste should also be obvious. And yet, apart from some scintillating exceptions, the leading figures in our community have evinced no genuine understanding for the needs of scholarship and what it takes to create a scholarly milieu and apparatus. They may loudly proclaim the need for an intensification of Jewish education, but they will not provide the funds for the very forum most likely to reach the Jewish youth of today and most likely to attract them, by sheer cultivation of interest in their own past, to deeper and more discriminating attachment to their historic heritage. Indeed, even organizations committed to support of Jewish community endeavors, which have made the stimulation of Jewish identity part of their explicit organizational commitment, have been quicker to invest in urban renewal and to provide more generous support for educational programs of ethnic minorities—of which the Jews have ceased to be one!—than they have for deeper and broader university programs of Judaica in this country. Alas, the people of the book are today far more enchanted by *The Source* and *Goodbye, Columbus* than they are by the *Proceedings of the American Academy for Jewish Research* or the Yale Judaica Series. That, I suppose, is no more than we should expect from the vulgus, but it is not a situation that we can afford to watch complacently.

While there are many deep-rooted causes for this state of affairs, there is one which I think we cannot afford to overlook, for in long-range terms we are capable of effecting some improvement. Few of us ever pay much attention to the crying need for administrators and communal executives who are profoundly oriented to Jewish culture. Oh yes, we bemoan their apathy and unsympathetic reception when we encounter them, but we hardly do anything about it. One reason for this, it seems to me, is that we have hardly ever represented administration in the field of Jewish education as a worthy pursuit. I do not mean principals of Hebrew schools, managers of bureaus of Jewish education, or Jewish social workers alone. I mean the growing need for deans and directors of programs of research as well as foundation administrators. Anyone who has had any experience with the problem of recruitment of librarians, directors of Jewish research projects, educational administrators—men who are not only charged with running things but with planning and financing—knows how much we have paid by way of our apathy. Among the destructive intellectual baggage we have inherited from our Jewish legacy—reinforced, to be sure, by the campus atmosphere generally—is the sentiment that creative men become teachers and scholars. Those who are played out but can affect Madison Avenue style should become deans. Need I say more? How to correct this quickly, I do not know. But it is clear that our attitude must change and that we cannot abdicate responsibility for attitudes that will in large measure affect the shape of our profession and discipline in the future. At least initiatory consideration of this matter of grave practical consequence seems to me to be warranted by a responsible group of educators.

*   *   *

We are a young group of scholars already endowed with many sorts of riches—poets, students, a sympathetic environment and greater physical resources than Jewish scholars have ever had before. We could easily fall prey to the temptation to discuss abstract questions that are never solved and have no immediate consequence. I am not unaware that I have touched on far too many problems for one discussion and that some of them will be with us for many years to come. I would hope, however, that they are questions that are of vital concern to each of us in his daily work and that together we can begin to do something about meeting them.

PARTICIPANTS IN THE COLLOQUIUM ON THE TEACHING OF JUDAICA IN AMERICAN UNIVERSITIES

September 7–10, 1969

Walter Ackerman, University of Judaism
Alexander Altmann, Brandeis University
Arnold Band, University of California
Isaac Barzillai, Columbia University
Charles Berlin, Harvard College Library
Lawrence Berman, Stanford University
Joseph Blau, Columbia University
Gerald Blidstein, Temple University
Harry Bracken, McGill University
Gerson Cohen, Columbia University
Robert Chazan, Ohio State University
Lucy Dawidowicz, Yeshiva University
Daniel Elazar, Temple University
Seymour Feldman, Rutgers University
Henry Fischel, University of Indiana
Edward Fox, Cornell University
Marvin Fox, Ohio State University
Lloyd Gartner, City University of New York
Nahum Glatzer, Brandeis University
Bernard Goldstein, Yale University
Irving Greenberg, Yeshiva University
Moshe Greenberg, University of Pennsylvania

William Hallo, Yale University
Benjamin Halpern, Brandeis University
Marvin Herzog, Columbia University
Alfred Ivry, Cornell University
Leon A. Jick, Brandeis University
Milton Konvitz, Cornell University
Samuel Leiter, Jewish Theological Seminary .
Baruch A. Levine, New York University
Joseph Lukinsky, Brandeis University
Michael Meyer, Hebrew Union College-Jewish Institute of Religion
Yochanan Muffs, Jewish Theological Seminary
Jacob Neusner, Brown University
Bezalel Porten, University of California
Ellis Rivkin, Hebrew Union College-Jewish Institute of Religion
Natan Rotenstreich, Hebrew University
Nahum Sarna, Brandeis University
Marshall Sklare, Yeshiva University
Louis Schoffman, Brooklyn College
Ismar Schorsch, Columbia University
Lou Silberman, Vanderbilt University
Morton Smith, Columbia University
Frank Talmage, Toronto University
Mervin Verbit, Brooklyn College
Jochanan Wijnhoven, Smith College
Yosef Yerushalmi, Harvard University

OBSERVERS

Harry Barron, National Foundation for Jewish Culture
Daniel Cohen, The State University of New York
Leonard Fein, Massachusetts Institute of Technology
Samuel Fox, Merrimack College
Abraham Gannes, The Jewish Agency
Paul Ritterband, Columbia University
David Weinstein, College of Jewish Studies, Chicago